MYSTERIES

OF THE

ROSARY

Joyful, Luminous, Sorrowful and Glorious Mysteries

Anne Catherine Emmerich

Arranged and Edited By
Ryan Grant

TAN Books
Gastonia, North Carolina

Cover & interior design by www.davidferrisdesign.com

Image Credits: Cover: *Our Lady of the Rosary*, CB Chambers, Restored Traditions, Pg. 4: Luis Juárez, *The Annunciation*, Museo Nacional de Arte (Public domain) Google Art Project, Wikimedia Commons, Pg. 30: Andrea del Verrocchio, Leonardo Da Vinci, *Baptism of Christ*, (Public domain), via Wikimedia Commons https://commons.wikimedia.org /wiki/File:Andrea_del_Verrocchio,_Leonardo_da_Vinci_-_Baptism_of_Christ_-_Uffizi .jpg., Pg. 62: El Greco, *The Agony in the Garden of Gethsemane*, National Gallery, London (Public domain), Wikimedia Commons, Pg. 94: Ricci, Sebastiano, *The Resurrection*, Dulwich Picture Gallery (Public domain) Google Art Project, Wikimedia Commons, Pg. 124: Giovanni Battista Salvi da Sassoferrato, *The Virgin in Prayer*, National Gallery, London (Public domain), Wikimedia Commons, Pg. 129: Rosary graphic from *How to Say the Rosary Leaflet*, TAN Books.

ISBN: 978-1-5051-1382-2

Published in the United States by

TAN Books
PO Box 269
Gastonia, NC 28053

www.TANBooks.com

Printed and bound in India

Contents

THE GLORIOUS MYSTERIES

HOW TO PRAY THE ROSARY

INTRODUCTION

THE MOST HOLY ROSARY is one of the greatest prayers in the history of the Church. Garnished as it is with the testimony of saints and popes for the last thousand years, the only prayers that could be said to be greater are those of the Mass and the Divine Office. Yet, many still seek ways to enter into the deeper mansions of spiritual richness to be found in this devotion.

Pope Leo XIII, whose papal magisterium did so much to popularize and spread the devotion of the Rosary, teaches us:

> As the various mysteries present themselves one after the other in the formula of the Rosary for the meditation and contemplation of men's minds, they also elucidate what we owe to Mary for our reconciliation and salvation. ... Now Christ stands forth clearly in the Rosary. We behold in meditation His life, whether His hidden life in joy, or His public life in excessive toil and sufferings unto death, or His glorious life from His triumphant resurrection to His eternal enthronement at the right hand of the Father. (*Fidentem Piumque Animum*, 1896)

1

The challenge then, has been focusing on the mysteries to better follow the life of our Lord through the eyes of Our Blessed Lady. To this end, many books have been produced over the years, employing various methods of meditation. What we have produced here stands out from them as a unique work, which has arranged the mysteries of the Rosary through the eyes of the great mystic, Blessed Anne Catherine Emmerich.

Blessed Anne Catherine was a mystic who experienced many marvelous private revelations concerning events of the Old and New Testaments, and provides many details that we do not find in the Scripture. Here, however, it is necessary to affirm that these private revelations are just that—they do not have an equal status to Divine Revelation which constitutes Sacred Scripture and the Deposit of Faith handed down by the Apostles. The Church merely affirms that they are free from error in faith and morals. One may wonder, if these are not absolutely certain, or an addendum to Scripture, why do we have them? The answer is to direct our actions more precisely to the love and knowledge of Jesus Christ, which is the very purpose of the Most Holy Rosary. As St. Thomas Aquinas teaches, "At all times there have not been lacking persons having the spirit of prophecy, not indeed for the declaration of any new doctrine of faith, but for the direction of human acts" (*II IIæ*, q. 174, a. 6, ad 3). When a private revelation is given, the light and inspiration comes from God, but uses the material present in the mind of the visionary to build and establish the revelation to focus once more upon devotion.

Therefore, even if one need not give the assent of faith to the precise historicity of the visions of Blessed Anne Catherine (which no authority has ever suggested), it is more than enough to focus on the love of Jesus Christ fostered through prayerful study of these pages.

Thus, our purpose here is to provide the reader with excerpts from Blessed Anne Catherine's visions to direct their acts of meditation more completely on the mysteries of Jesus contained in the rosary. One may read *Mysteries of the Rosary* as a book so as to provide more fruitful details for meditation later, or for meditation while praying the rosary.

—The Editor

THE
JOYFUL
MYSTERIES

* 1 *

THE ANNUNCIATION

And the angel having come in, said unto her:
Hail, full of grace, the Lord is with you:
blessed are you among women.

LUKE 1:27-28

I saw the Blessed Virgin a short time after her marriage in the house of Nazareth. Joseph was not there. He was at that moment journeying with two beasts of burden on the road to Tiberias, to which he was going to get his tools. But Anne was in the house with her maid and two of the virgins who had been with Mary in the Temple. Everything in the house had been newly arranged by Anne. Toward evening, they all prayed standing... around a circular stool from which they afterward ate vegetables that had been served. Anne seemed to be very busy about the household affairs, and for a time she

7

moved around here and there, while the Blessed Virgin ascended the steps to her room.

Mary laid a small, round cushion on the floor and she gently sank on her knees, her back turned to her couch, the door of the chamber to her right. Mary lowered her veil over her face, and folded her hands upon her chest. I saw her praying for a long time with intense fervor. She prayed for Redemption, for the promised King, and that her own supplications might have some influence upon His coming. She knelt long, as if in ecstasy, her face raised to Heaven; then she drooped her head upon her chest and thus continued her prayer. And now she glanced to the right and beheld a radiant youth with flowing, yellow hair. It was the archangel Gabriel. His feet did not touch the ground. In an oblique line and surrounded by an effulgence of light and glory, he came floating down to Mary. The lamp grew dim, for the whole room was lit up by the glory. The angel, with hands gently raised before his breast, spoke to Mary. I saw the words like letters of glittering light issuing from his lips. Mary replied, but without looking up. Then the angel again spoke and Mary, as if in obedience to his command, raised her veil a little, glanced at him, and said, "Behold the handmaid of the Lord. May it be done unto me according to your word!" I saw her now in deeper ecstasy. The ceiling of the room vanished, and over the house appeared a luminous cloud with a pathway of light leading up from it to the opened heavens. Far up in the source of this light, I beheld a vision of the Most Holy Trinity.

As Mary uttered the words: "May it be done unto me according to your word!" I saw an apparition of the Holy Spirit. The countenance was human and the whole apparition environed by dazzling splendor, as if surrounded by wings. From the chest and hands, I saw issuing three streams of light. They penetrated the right side of the Blessed Virgin and united into one under her heart. At that instant Mary became perfectly transparent and luminous. It was as if opacity disappeared like darkness before that flood of light.

While the angel and the streams of glory vanished, I saw down the path of light that led up to Heaven, showers of half-blown roses and tiny green leaves falling upon Mary. She, entirely absorbed in self, saw in herself the Incarnate Son of God, a tiny, human form of light with all the members, even to the little fingers, perfect. Mary knew that she had conceived the Redeemer, yes, her interior lay open before her, and so she already understood that her Son's kingdom should be a supernatural one, and that the House of Jacob, the Church, would be the reunion of regenerate mankind.

She knew that the Redeemer would be the King of His people, that He would purify them and render them victorious; but that in order to redeem them He must suffer and die. It was explained to me likewise why the Redeemer remained nine months in His mother's womb, why He was born a little child and not a perfect man like Adam, and why also He did not take the beauty of Adam in Paradise. The Incarnate Son of God willed to be conceived and born that conception and birth, rendered so very unholy by the Fall, might again become holy. Mary was His Mother, and He did not come sooner because Mary was the first and the only woman conceived without sin.

✝ ✝ ✝

We offer You, O Lord Jesus, this first
decade in honor of Your Incarnation
in Mary's womb, and we ask of You,
through this mystery and through her
intercession, a profound humility.
Amen.

Our Father, 10 Hail Marys,
Glory Be, Oh my Jesus.

May the grace of the Mystery of the
Annunciation come down into
our souls. Amen.

* 2 *

THE VISITATION

And Elizabeth was filled with the Holy Ghost:
And she cried out with a loud voice, and said:
"Blessed are you among women,
and blessed is the fruit of your womb."

LUKE 1:42-43

After the Conception of Jesus, the Blessed Virgin experienced a great desire to visit her cousin Elizabeth. I saw her travelling with Joseph toward the south to Zachary's house; it was a journey of about twelve hours. Near Jerusalem they turned off to the north in order to take a more solitary route. They made the circuit of a little city two leagues from Emmaus, and took a road traversed by Jesus in after years. Although it was a long journey, they made it very quickly.

Zachary's house stood upon a solitary hill, and other dwellings were scattered around. Not far from it, a tolerably large brook flowed down from the mountain. Elizabeth had learned in vision that one of her race was to give birth to the Messiah; she had dwelt in thought upon Mary, had very greatly desired to see her, and had indeed beheld her journeying to Hebron. In a little room, to the right of the entrance to the house, she placed seats, and here she tarried, often looking long and anxiously down the road, in the hope of catching the first glimpse of Mary. When Zachary was returning from the Passover, I saw Elizabeth, urged by an impetuous desire, hurrying from the house and going a considerable distance on the road to Jerusalem. When Zachary met her, he was alarmed to find her so far from home and that, too, in her present condition. But she told him of her anxiety and that she could not help thinking that her cousin Mary was coming from Nazareth to see her.

Zachary, however, thought it improbable that the newly married couple would at that time undertake so great a journey. On the following day, I saw Elizabeth taking the road again under the influence of the same impression, and now I saw the Holy Family coming to meet her. As soon as the Blessed Virgin saw Elizabeth, she recognized her and hurried on to meet her, while Joseph purposely held back.

When the cousins met, they saluted each other joyfully with outstretched hands. I saw a light in Mary and, issuing from her, a ray which entered into Elizabeth, who thereby became wonderfully excited. They did not pause long in sight of the beholders, but arm in arm passed up the courtyard to the door of the house, where Elizabeth once more bade Mary welcome.

Joseph went around to the side of the house and into an open hall where sat Zachary. He respectfully saluted the aged priest, who responded in writing on his tablet. Mary and Elizabeth entered the room in which was the fireplace. Here they embraced, clasping each other in their arms and pressing cheek to cheek. I saw light streaming down between them. Then it was that Elizabeth, becoming interiorly inflamed, stepped back with uplifted hands, and exclaimed,

> "Blessed are you among women, and blessed is the Fruit of your womb.

> "And how is it, that the Mother of my Lord should come to me?

> "For behold, as soon as the voice of your greeting sounded in my ears, the infant in my womb leaped for joy.

> "And blessed are you who believed, because those things shall be accomplished that were spoken to you by the Lord."

At these last words, Elizabeth took Mary into the little room prepared for her that she might sit down and rest. It was only a few steps from where they then were. Mary released her hold upon Elizabeth's arm, crossed her hands on her chest, and divinely inspired, uttered her canticle of thanksgiving:

"My soul magnifies the Lord, and my spirit has rejoiced in God, my Savior.

"Because He has regarded the humility of His handmaid; for behold from henceforth all generations shall call me blessed.

"Because He who is mighty has done great things to me: and holy is His name.

"And His mercy is from generation unto generations, to those who fear Him.

"He has showed might in His arm: He has scattered the proud in the conceit of their heart.

"He has put down the mighty from their seat, and has exalted the humble.

"He has filled the hungry with good things: and the rich He has sent empty away.

"He has received Israel his servant, being mindful of His mercy.

"As He spoke to our fathers, to Abraham, and to His seed forever."

I saw Elizabeth, moved by similar emotion, reciting the whole canticle with Mary. The Blessed Virgin remained with Elizabeth three months, until after the birth of John, but she returned to Nazareth before his circumcision.

+ + +

We offer You, O Lord Jesus, this
second decade in honor of the
Visitation of Your holy Mother to her
cousin
St. Elizabeth and the sanctification of
St. John the Baptist, and we ask of You,
through this mystery and through the
intercession of Your holy Mother,
charity toward our neighbor. Amen.

Our Father, 10 Hail Marys,
Glory Be, O my Jesus.

May the grace of the Mystery of the
Visitation come down into
our souls. Amen.

* 3 *

THE NATIVITY

And it came to pass, that when they were there, her days were accomplished, that she should be delivered. And she brought forth her firstborn son, and wrapped him up in swaddling clothes, and laid him in a manger; because there was no room for them in the inn.

LUKE 2:6-7

I saw Joseph arranging a seat and couch for Mary in the so-called Suckling Cave of Abraham, which was also the sepulcher of Maraha, his nurse. It was more spacious than the cave of the Crib. Mary remained there some hours, while Joseph was making the latter more habitable. He brought also from the city many different little vessels and some dried fruits. Mary told him that the birth hour of the Child would arrive on the coming night. It was then nine months since her conception by the Holy Spirit. She begged him to do all in his power that they might receive

16

as honorably as possible this Child promised by God, this Child supernaturally conceived; and she invited him to unite with her in prayer for those hard-hearted people who would afford Him no place of shelter. Although Joseph proposed to bring some pious women whom he knew in Bethlehem to her assistance, Mary would not allow it. She declared that she had no need of anyone.

It was five o'clock in the evening when Joseph brought Mary back again to the Crib Cave. He hung up several more lamps, and made a place under the shed before the door for the little donkey, which came joyfully hurrying from the fields to meet them. When Mary told Joseph that her time was drawing near and that he should now retire for prayer, he left her and turned toward his sleeping place to do her bidding. Before entering his little recess, he looked back once toward that part of the cave where Mary knelt upon her couch in prayer, her back to him, her face toward the east. He saw the cave filled with the light that streamed from Mary, for she was completely enveloped as if by flames. It was as if he were, like Moses, looking into the burning bush. He sank prostrate to the ground in prayer, and looked not back again. The glory around Mary became brighter and brighter, the lamps that Joseph had lit were no longer to be seen. Mary knelt, her flowing white robe spread out before her. At the twelfth hour, her prayer became ecstatic, and I saw her raised so far above the ground that one could see it beneath her. Her hands were crossed upon her chest, and the light around her grew even more resplendent. I no longer saw the roof of the cave.

Above Mary stretched a pathway of light up to Heaven, in which pathway it seemed as if one light came forth from another, as if one figure dissolved into another, and from these different spheres of light other heavenly figures issued. Mary continued in prayer, her eyes bent low upon the ground. At that moment she gave birth to the Infant Jesus. I saw Him like a tiny, shining Child, lying on the rug at her knees, and brighter far than all the other brilliancy. Even inanimate nature seemed stirred. The stones of the rocky floor and the walls of the cave were glimmering and sparkling, as if alive with instinct. Mary's ecstasy lasted some moments longer. Then I saw her spread a cover over the Child, but she did not yet take Him up, nor even touch Him. After a long time, I saw the Child stirring and heard Him crying, and then only did Mary seem to recover full consciousness. She lifted the Child, along with the cover that she had thrown over Him, to her breast and sat veiled, herself and Child quite enveloped. I saw angels around her in human form prostrate on their faces.

It may, perhaps, have been an hour after the birth when Mary called St. Joseph, who still lay prostrate in prayer. When he approached, he fell on his knees, his face to the ground, in a transport of joy, devotion, and humility. Mary urged him to look upon the Sacred Gift from Heaven, and then did Joseph take the Child into his arms. And now the Blessed Virgin swathed the Child in red and over that in a white veil up as far as under the little arms, and the upper part of the body from the armpits to the head, she wrapped up in another piece of linen. She laid the Child in the Crib, which had been filled with rushes and fine moss over which was spread a cover that hung down at the sides. When Mary laid the Child in the Crib, both she and Joseph stood by Him in tears, singing the praises of God.

On the night of the Birth there gushed forth a beautiful spring in the other cave that lay to the right. The water ran out, and the next day Joseph dug a course for it and formed a spring. I saw extraordinary gladness in many places, even in the most distant regions of the world, something marvelous on that midnight. By it the good were filled with joyful longings, and the bad with dread. I saw also many of the lower animals joyfully exited. I saw fountains gushing forth and swelling, flowers springing up in many places, trees and plants budding with new life, and all sending forth their fragrance. I saw the three eldest shepherds, roused by the wonders of the night, standing together before their huts, gazing around and pointing out the magnificent light that shone over the Crib. I saw something like a cloud of glory descend upon the three shepherds, and heard the approach of sweet, clear voices singing softly.

At first, the shepherds were frightened. Soon there stood before them five or seven lovely, radiant figures holding in their hands a long strip like a scroll upon which were written words in letters a hand in length. The angels were singing the *Gloria*. The three shepherds went to the Crib early next morning.

I saw that Anne at Nazareth, Elizabeth in Juttah, Noemi, Anna, and Simeon in the Temple—all had on this night visions from which they learned the birth of the Savior. The child John was unspeakably joyous. But only Anne knew where the newborn Child was; the others, and even Elizabeth, knew indeed of Mary and saw her in vision, but they knew nothing of Bethlehem.

✝ ✝ ✝

We offer You, O Lord Jesus, this third
decade in honor of Your Nativity in
the stable of Bethlehem, and we ask of
You, through this mystery and through
the intercession of Your holy Mother,
detachment from the things of the
world, contempt of riches and
love of poverty. Amen.

Our Father, 10 Hail Marys,
Glory Be, O my Jesus.

May the grace of the Mystery of the
Nativity come down into
our souls. Amen.

* 4 *

THE PRESENTATION
IN THE TEMPLE

And Simeon blessed them, and said to Mary his mother:
"Behold this child is set for the fall, and for the resurrection
of many in Israel, and for a sign which shall be contradicted;
And your own soul a sword shall pierce, that, out of many
hearts, thoughts may be revealed."

LUKE 2:34-35

I saw the Holy Family accompanied by the two old people going into the city and to the Temple. The donkey was laden as if for a journey, and they had with them the basket of offerings. They first entered a court that was surrounded by a wall, and there the donkey was tied under a shed. The Blessed Virgin and Child were received by an old woman and conducted along a covered walk up to the Temple. The old woman carried a light, for it was still dark. Here in this passage came Simeon full of expectation

21

to meet Mary. He spoke a few joyous words with her, took the Child Jesus, pressed Him to his heart, and then hurried to another side of the Temple. Since the preceding evening, when he had received the announcement of the angel, he had been consumed by desire. He had taken his stand in the women's passage to the Temple, hardly able to await the coming of Mary and her Child. Mary was now led by the woman to a porch in that part of the Temple in which the ceremony of presentation was to take place. Anna and another woman (Noemi, Mary's former directress) received her. Simeon came out to the porch and conducted Mary with the Child in her arms into the hall to the right of the women's porch. It was in this porch that the treasure box stood by which Jesus was sitting when the widow cast in her mite. Old Anna, to whom Joseph had handed over the basket of fruit and doves, followed with Noemi, and Joseph retired to the standing place of the men.

Simeon conducted Mary through the altar rail and up to the table of sacrifice. The Infant Jesus, wrapped in His sky-blue dress, was laid in the basket cradle. Mary wore a sky-blue dress, a white veil, and a long, yellowish mantle. When the Child had been placed in the cradle, Simeon led Mary out again to the standing place of the women. He then proceeded to the altar proper, whereon lay the priestly vestments and at which, besides himself, three other priests were vesting. And now one of them went behind, one before, and two on either side of the table, and prayed over the Child, while Anna approached Mary, gave her the doves and fruit in two little baskets, one on top of the other, and went with her to the altar rail.

Anna remained there while Mary, led again by Simeon, passed on through the railing and up to the altar. There upon one of the dishes she deposited the fruit, and into the other laid some coins; the doves she placed upon the table in the basket. Simeon stood before the table near Mary while the priest behind it took the Child from the cradle, raised Him on high and toward the different parts of the Temple, praying all the while. Simeon next received the Child from him, laid Him in Mary's arms, and, from a roll of parchment that lay near him on a desk, prayed over her and the Child.

After that Simeon again led Mary to the railing, whence Anna accompanied her to the place set apart for the women. In the meantime, about twenty mothers with their firstborn had arrived. Joseph and several others were standing back in the place assigned to the men.

Then two priests at the altar proper began a religious service accompanied by incense and prayers. When these ceremonies were ended, Simeon went to where Mary was standing, took the Child into his arms and, entranced with joy, spoke long and loud. When he ceased, Anna, also filled with the Spirit, spoke a long time. I saw that the people around heard them and all were deeply impressed, and regarded Mary and the Child with great reverence. Mary shone like a rose.

I did not witness the purification ceremonies of the other mothers; but I had an interior conviction that all the children offered on that day would receive special grace, and that some of the martyred innocents were among them.

When the Most Holy Child Jesus was laid upon the altar in the basket cradle, an indescribable light filled the Temple. I saw that God was in that light, and I saw the heavens open up as far as the Most Holy Trinity.

✝ ✝ ✝

We offer You, O Lord Jesus, this fourth decade in honor of Your Presentation in the Temple and the Purification of Mary, and we ask of You, through this mystery and through the intercession of Your holy Mother, purity of body and soul. Amen.

Our Father, 10 Hail Marys, Glory Be, O my Jesus.

May the grace of the Mystery of the Presentation in the Temple come down into our souls. Amen.

* 5 *

THE FINDING
IN THE TEMPLE

After three days, they found him in the temple,
sitting in the midst of the doctors,
hearing them, and asking them questions.
And all who heard him were astonished
at his wisdom and his answers.

LUKE 2:46-47

At the age of eight years, Jesus went for the first time with His parents to Jerusalem for the Pasch, and every succeeding year He did the same. In those first visits, Jesus had already excited attention in Jerusalem among the friends with whom He and His parents stayed, also among the priests and doctors. They spoke of the pious, intelligent Child, of Joseph's extraordinary Son, just as amongst us one might, at the annual pilgrimages, notice in particular this or that modest, holy-looking person, this or that clever peasant child, and recognize him again the next year. So Jesus had already some acquaintances in the city when, in His twelfth year, with their friends and their sons, He accompanied His parents to Jerusalem. His parents were accustomed to walk with the people from their own part of the country, and they knew that Jesus, who now made the journey for the fifth time, always went with the other youths from Nazareth.

But this time Jesus had, on the return journey not far from the Mount of Olives, separated from His companions, who all thought that He had joined His parents who were following. Mary and Joseph thought Him on ahead with the other Nazarenes, while these latter thought that He was following with His parents. When at last they all met at Gophna, the anxiety of Mary and Joseph at His absence was very great. They returned at once to Jerusalem, making inquiries after Him on the way and everywhere in the city itself. But they could not find Him, since He had not been where they usually stayed. Jesus had slept at the inn before the Bethlehem gate, where the people knew Him and His parents.

There He had joined several youths and gone with them to two schools of the city, the first day to one, the second to another. On the morning of the third day, He had gone to a third school at the Temple, and in the afternoon into the Temple itself where His parents found Him.

Jesus by His questions and answers so astonished and embarrassed the doctors and rabbis of all these schools that they resolved, on the afternoon of the third day, in the public lecture hall of the Temple and in presence of the rabbis most deeply versed in the various sciences "to humble the Boy Jesus."

The scribes and doctors had concerted the plan together; for, although pleased at first, they had in the end become vexed at Him. They met in the public lecture hall in the middle of the Temple porch in front of the Sanctuary, in the round place where later Jesus also taught. There I saw Jesus sitting in a large chair; around Him was a crowd of aged Jews in priestly robes. They were listening attentively, and appeared to be perfectly furious. As Jesus had in the schools illustrated His answers and explanations by all kinds of examples from nature, art, and science, the scribes and doctors had diligently gathered together masters in all these branches. They now began, one by one, to dispute with Him.

He remarked that although, properly speaking, such subjects did not appear appropriate to the Temple, yet He would discuss them since such was His Father's will. But they understood not that He referred to His Heavenly Father; they imagined that Joseph had commanded Him to show off His learning. Jesus now answered and taught upon medicine. He described the whole human body in a way far beyond the reach of even the most learned. He discoursed with the same facility upon astronomy, architecture, agriculture, geometry, arithmetic, jurisprudence and, in fine, upon every subject proposed to Him. He applied all so skillfully to the Law and the Promise, to the

Prophecies, to the Temple, to the mysteries of worship and sacrifice that His hearers, surprised and confounded, passed successively from astonishment and admiration to fury and shame. They were enraged at hearing some things that they never before knew, and at hearing others that they had never before understood.

Jesus had been teaching two hours, when Joseph and Mary entered the Temple. They inquired after their Child of the Levites whom they knew, and received for answer that He was with the doctors in the lecture hall. But as they were not at liberty to enter that hall, they sent one of the Levites in to call Jesus. Jesus sent them word that He must first finish what He was then about. Mary was very much troubled at His not obeying at once, for this was the first time He had given His parents to understand that He had other commands than theirs to fulfill.

He continued to teach for another hour, and then He left the hall and joined His parents in the porch of Israel, the women's porch, leaving His hearers bewildered, confused, and enraged.

Joseph was quite awed and astonished, but he kept a humble silence. Mary, however, drawing near to Jesus, said, "Child, why have You done this to us? Behold, Your father and I have sought You with great sorrow!" But Jesus answered gravely, "Why have you sought Me? Do you not know that I must be about My Father's business?" But they did not understand. They at once began with Him their journey home. The bystanders gazed at them in astonishment; although the crowd was dense, yet a wide path was made to permit the Holy Family to pass.

Jesus' teaching made a great impression upon the scribes. Some recorded the affair as a notable event, while here and there it was whispered around, giving rise to all kinds of remarks and false reports. But the true statement, the scribes kept to themselves. They spoke of Jesus as of a very forward boy, possessed indeed of fine talents, but said those talents required cultivation.

We offer You, O Lord Jesus, this fifth
decade in honor of Mary's finding You
in the Temple, and we ask of You,
through this mystery and through her
intercession, the gift of true wisdom.
Amen.

*Our Father, 10 Hail Marys,
Glory Be, O my Jesus.*

May the grace of the Mystery of the
Finding of Our Lord in the Temple
come down into our souls. Amen.

THE
LUMINOUS
MYSTERIES

* 1 *

THE BAPTISM OF JESUS

And Jesus being baptized, forthwith came out of the water:
and lo, the heavens were opened to him: and he saw the
Spirit of God descending as a dove, and coming upon him.
And behold a voice from heaven, saying: "This is my
beloved Son, in whom I am well pleased."

MATTHEW 3:16-17

A crowd more numerous than usual was assembled to whom John was with great animation preaching of the nearness of the Messiah and of penance, proclaiming at the same time that the moment was approaching for him to retire from his office of teacher. Jesus was standing in the throng of listeners. John felt His presence. He saw Him also, and that fired him with zeal and filled his heart with joy. But he did not on that account interrupt his discourse, and when he had finished he began to baptize.

He had already baptized very many and it was drawing

on to ten o'clock, when Jesus in His turn came down among the aspirants to the pool of baptism.

John bowed low before Him, saying: "I ought to be baptized by You, and You come to me?" Jesus answered: "Suffer it to be so now, for so it behooves us to fulfill all justice that you baptize Me and I be baptized by you." He said also: "You shall receive the baptism of the Holy Spirit and of blood."

Then John begged Him to follow him to the island. Jesus replied that He would do so, provided that some of the water with which all were baptized should be poured into the basin, that all present should be baptized at the same place with Himself, and that the tree by which He was to support Himself should be transplanted to the ordinary place of baptism, that all might share the same conveniences.

The Savior now went with John and His two disciples, Andrew and Saturnin. The disciples followed the Lord to the island where at the far end of the bridge the people stood on the shore in great crowds.

On the bridge itself three could stand abreast. One of the foremost in the latter position was Lazarus. They crossed the bridge to the island and into a little tent that, close to the eastern edge of the baptismal well, had been erected for the purpose of robing and disrobing.

The baptismal well lay in a gently inclined, octangular basin the bottom of which was encircled by a similarly shaped rim connected with the Jordan by five subterranean canals. The water surrounded the whole basin, filling it through incisions made in the rim, three in the northern side serving as inlets, and two on the southern acting as outlets.

Jesus entered the tent and there laid off, first, His mantle and girdle. Retaining His brown, woven undergarment, He stepped forth and descended to the margin of the well, where He drew it off over His head. About His loins was fastened a broad linen band which was also wound around each limb for about half a foot. Saturnin received the garments of the Lord as He disrobed, and handed them to Lazarus, who was standing on the edge of the island.

And now Jesus descended into the well, and stood in the water up to His chest. His left arm encircled the tree, His right hand was laid on His chest, and the loosened ends of the white, linen binder floated out on the water.

On the southern side of the well stood John, holding in his hand a shell with a perforated margin through which the water flowed in three streams. He stooped, filled the shell, and then poured the water in three streams over the head of the Lord, one on the back of the head, one in the middle, and the third over the forepart of the head and on the face.

While Jesus ascended from the depths of the baptismal well, Andrew and Saturnin put on Him a long, white baptismal robe. After this Jesus stepped on the red triangular stone which lay to the right of the descent into the well. Andrew and Saturnin each laid one hand upon His shoulder, while John rested his upon His head.

This part of the ceremony over, they were just about mounting the steps when the voice of God came over

Jesus, who was still standing alone and in prayer upon the stone. There came from Heaven a great, rushing wind like thunder. All trembled and looked up. A cloud of white light descended, and I saw over Jesus a winged figure of light as if flowing over Him like a stream. The heavens opened, I beheld an apparition of the Heavenly Father in the figure in which He is usually depicted and, in a voice of thunder, I heard the words: "This is My beloved Son in whom I am well pleased." Jesus was perfectly transparent, entirely penetrated by light; one could scarcely look at Him. I saw angels around Him.

But off at some distance on the waters of the Jordan, I saw Satan, a dark, black figure, as if in a cloud, and myriads of horrible black reptiles and vermin swarming around him. It was as if all the wickedness, all the sins, all the poison of the whole region took a visible form at the outpouring of the Holy Spirit, and fled into that dark figure as into their original source. The sight was abominable, but it served to heighten the effect of the indescribable splendor and joy and brilliancy spread over the Lord and the whole island.

The sacred baptismal well sparkled and glanced, foundations and margin and waters—a pool of living light. One could see the four stones that had once supported the Ark of the Covenant shining beneath the waters as if in exultation; and on the twelve around the well, those upon which the Levites had stood, appeared angels bending in adoration, for the Spirit of God had before all mankind rendered testimony to the living Foundation, to the precious, chosen Cornerstone of the Church around whom we as so many living stones, must build up a spiritual edifice, a holy priesthood, that thereby we may offer an acceptable, spiritual sacrifice to God through His beloved Son in whom He is well pleased.

Jesus then ascended the steps and entered the tent near the baptismal well. When clothed, He left the tent and, surrounded by His disciples, took His stand on the open space near the central tree. John in joyous tones addressed the crowd and bore witness to Jesus that He was the Son of God and the promised Messiah.

We offer You, O Lord Jesus, this first decade in honor of John's baptizing You, and we ask of You, through this mystery and through Mary's intercession,
the gift of Faith. Amen.

Our Father, 10 Hail Marys,
Glory Be, O my Jesus.

May the grace of the Mystery of the Baptism of Our Lord come down into our souls. Amen.

* 2 *

THE WEDDING
AT CANA

*And the wine failing, the mother of Jesus says to him:
"They have no wine." And Jesus says to her:
"Woman, what is that to me and to you? my hour
has not yet come." His mother says to the waiters:
"Do whatsoever he will say to you."*

JOHN 2:3-5

When Jesus with His disciples arrived near Cana, He was most deferentially received by Mary, the bride's parents, the bridegroom, and others that had come out to meet Him. All the relatives of St. Anne and Joachim had come from around Galilee to Cana, in all over one hundred guests. Mary Marcus, John Marcus, Obed, and Veronica had come from Jerusalem. Jesus Himself brought about twenty-five of His disciples with Him. Jesus' participation in this marriage, like every other action of His

earthly career, had, besides its high, mysterious significa-
tion, its exterior, apparent, and ordinary motives. More
than once had Mary sent messengers to Jesus begging Him
to be present at it. The friends and relatives of the Holy
Family, judging from a human view, were making such
speeches as these: "Mary, the Mother of Jesus, is a lone
widow. Jesus is roaming the country, caring little for her
or His relatives, etc., etc." It was on this account, therefore, that Mary was anxious that her Son should honor
His friends by His presence at the marriage.

Jesus entered into Mary's views and looked upon the
present as a fitting opportunity to disabuse them of their
erroneous ideas. He undertook also to supply one course
of the feast, and so Mary went to Cana before the other
guests and helped in the various preparations. Jesus had
engaged to supply all the wine for the feast, wherefore it
was that Mary so anxiously reminded Him that the wine
failed.

Jesus intended to manifest Himself at this feast to all
His friends and relatives. He wished also that all whom He
had chosen up to the present, should become known to
one another and to His own relatives. This could be done
with greater freedom on such an occasion as this marriage
festival. Jesus taught likewise in the synagogue before the
assembled guests. He spoke of the enjoyment of lawful
pleasures, of the motives through which they might be
indulged, and of the moderation and prudent reserve that
ought to accompany them. Then He spoke of marriage,

of husband and wife, of continence, of chastity, and of spiritual unions.

Jesus had engaged to supply the second course of the banquet as well as the wine, and for all this His Mother and Martha provided. This second course consisted of birds, fish, honey confections, fruits, and a kind of pastry which Veronica had brought with her. When it was all carried in and set on a side table, Jesus arose, gave the first cut to each dish, and then resumed His place at table. The dishes were served, but the wine failed. Jesus meanwhile was busy teaching. Now when the Blessed Virgin, who had provided for this part of the entertainment, saw that the wine failed, she went to Jesus and reminded Him that He had told her that He would see to the wine.

Jesus, who was teaching of His Heavenly Father, replied: "Woman, do not be anxious! Do not trouble yourself and Me! My hour has not yet come." These words were not uttered in harshness to the Blessed Virgin. Jesus addressed her as "Woman," and not as "Mother," because, at this moment as the Messiah, as the Son of God, He was present in divine power and was about to perform in the presence of all His disciples and relatives an action full of mystery.

On all occasions when He acted as the Incarnate Word, He ennobled those that participated in the same by giving them the title that best responded to the part assigned them. Thus did the holiness of the divine action shed, as it were, some rays upon them and communicate to them a special dignity.

Mary was the "Woman" who had brought forth Him whom now, as her Creator, she invokes on the occasion of the wine's failing. As the Creator, He will now give a proof of His high dignity. He will here show that He is the Son of God and not just the Son of Mary. Later on, when dying upon the Cross, He again addressed His weeping Mother by the appellation of Woman, "Woman, behold your son!" thereby designating John.

Jesus had promised His Mother that He would provide the wine. And here we see Mary beginning the role of mediatrix that she has ever since continued. She places before Him the failure of the wine. But the wine that He was about to provide was more than ordinary wine; it was symbolical of that mystery by which He would one day change wine into His own Blood. The reply: "My hour has not yet come," contained three significations: first, the hour for supplying the promised wine; secondly, the hour for changing water into wine, thirdly, the hour for changing wine into His own Blood.

But Mary's anxiety for the wedding guests was now entirely relieved. She had mentioned the matter to her Son, therefore she says confidently to the servants: "Do all that He tells you." Mary told the servants to await the commands of Jesus and fulfill them. After a little while Jesus directed them to bring Him the empty jugs and turn them upside down. Then Jesus ordered each to be filled with water. The servants took them off to the well which was in a vault in the cellar, and which consisted of a stone cistern provided with a pump. The jugs were earthen, large and so heavy that when full it took two men to carry them, one at each handle.

Mary's words to Jesus had been uttered in a low tone, but Jesus' reply, as well as His command to draw water, was given in a loud voice. When the jugs filled with water had been placed, six in number, on the side table, Jesus went and blessed them. As He retook His place at table, He called to a servant: "Draw off now, and bring a drink to the steward!"

When this latter had tasted the wine, he approached the bridegroom and said: "Every man at first sets forth good wine, and when men have well drunk, then that which is worse. But you have kept the good wine until now."

Then the bridegroom and the bride's father drank of the wine, and great was their astonishment. The servants protested that they had drawn only water, and that the drinking vessels and glasses on the table had been filled with the same. And now the whole company drank.

The miracle gave rise to no alarm or excitement; on the contrary, a spirit of silent awe and reverence fell upon them. Jesus taught much upon this miracle: He said that the world presents the strong wine first, and then deceives the partially intoxicated with bad drinks; but it was not so in the Kingdom that His Heavenly Father had given Him.

There pure water was changed to costly wine, as luke-warmness should give place to ardor and intrepid zeal. His listeners were filled with fear and wonder, and the wine produced a change in all. I saw that, not by the miracle alone, but also by the drinking of that wine, each one had received strength, true and interior, each had become changed. His disciples, His relatives, in a word, all present were now convinced of Jesus' power and dignity, as well as of His mission. All believed in Him.

Faith at once took possession of every heart. All became better, more united, more interior. This same effect was produced in all that had drunk of the wine. Jesus at this wedding feast was, as it were, in the midst of His community for the first time. There it was that He wrought that first miracle in their favor and for the confirmation of their faith. It is on that account that this miracle, the changing of water into wine, is recorded as the first in His history; as that of the Last Supper, when His Apostles were staunch in the Faith, was the last.

✝ ✝ ✝

We offer You, O Lord Jesus, this second decade in honor of the Wedding Feast, and we ask of You, through this mystery and through Mary's intercession,
the gift of fidelity. Amen.

*Our Father, 10 Hail Marys,
Glory Be, O my Jesus.*

May the grace of Our Lord's first miracle at the Wedding Feast come down into our souls. Amen.

* 3 *

PROCLAMATION
OF THE KINGDOM

And after John was delivered up, Jesus came into Galilee,
preaching the gospel of the kingdom of God,
And saying: "The time is accomplished,
and the kingdom of God is at hand: repent,
and believe the gospel."

MARK 1:14-15

Jesus then ascended the steps and entered the tent near
the baptismal well. Saturnin brought the garments which
Lazarus had been holding all this time, and Jesus put them
on. When clothed, He left the tent and, surrounded by
His disciples, took His stand on the open space near the
central tree. John in joyous tones addressed the crowd
and bore witness to Jesus that He was the Son of God and
the promised Messiah. He cited the Prophecies of the
Patriarchs and prophets now fulfilled, recounted what he

had seen, reminded them of the voice of God which they had heard, and informed them that when Jesus returned he himself would retire. John referred also to the sacred memories that embalmed the spot upon which they were standing on account of the Ark of the Covenant's having rested here when Israel was journeying to the Land of Promise. Now, he continued, had they seen the Realization of the Covenant witnessed to by His Father, the Almighty God Himself. John referred all to Jesus, and called this day that had beheld the fulfillment of the desire of Israel blessed. Meanwhile many newcomers had arrived on the spot, and among them some friends of Jesus. I saw in the crowd Nicodemus, Obed, Joseph of Arimathea, John Marc, and others. John bade Andrew announce the baptism of the Messiah throughout Galilee. Then Jesus spoke, confirming in plain and simple words the truth John had proclaimed. He told them that He would withdraw from them for a short time, after which all the sick and afflicted should come to Him and He would heal and console them. They should in the meantime prepare themselves by penance and good works. He would withdraw for awhile, and then return to lay the foundations of that Kingdom which His Father had given to Him. Jesus made use of a parable when thus addressing the crowd: that of a king's son who, before taking possession of his throne, withdrew into solitude, there to prepare himself and implore the assistance of his father.

Among His numerous listeners were some Pharisees, who received His words with ridicule. "Perhaps, after all," they said, "He is not the carpenter's son, but the supposititious child of some king. Is He now about to return to His kingdom? Will He assemble His subjects and march upon Jerusalem?" The idea appeared to them foolish and absurd. John recommenced his work, and continued throughout the whole day baptizing at the sacred well of Jesus all that were on the island. They were for the most part people who later on joined the Community of Jesus. They stepped into the water that covered the rim of the pool, the baptist standing outside on the edge itself baptizing. I remember that He spoke of the Children of Israel. After crossing the Red Sea, they had on account of their sins wandered so long in the desert, before being allowed to pass through the Jordan and into the Promised Land. Now was the actual fulfillment of what was then only typical, for the baptism in the Jordan had been symbolized by the passage of the Israelites through its waters. If they now remained true and observed God's commands, they should indeed be put into possession of the Promised Land and the City of God. Jesus spoke in a spiritual sense, signifying thereby the Heavenly Jerusalem. But His hearers dreamed only of an earthly kingdom and of deliverance from the Romans. Jesus then spoke of the Ark of the Covenant and of the severity of the Old Law, for whoever approached so near the Ark as to touch it instantly fell dead; but now was the Law fulfilled and grace poured forth in the Son of Man. Now, too, was being fulfilled that of which the angel's conducting Tobit back into the Promised

Land was a figure; for they who, faithful to the commands of God, had so long pined in captivity were now to be introduced into the freedom of the Law of grace. Jesus referred also to Judith, the widow, who had delivered Bethuel from oppression by cutting off the head of Holofernes, the Assyrian, as he lay sunk in the fumes of wine. Now would the Virgin, foreseen from eternity, become great and exalted, while the proud heads that had once oppressed Bethuel would fall. By this Jesus signified the Church and her triumph over the powers of the world.

When they approached Ophra, Jesus sent the nephews of Joseph of Arimathea on ahead, in order to get the key of the synagogue and to call the people to the instruction. Jesus always entrusted such messages to these youths, for they were very clever and amiable. At the entrance of the city, the possessed and lunatics ran around Jesus, crying out:

"Here comes the Prophet, the Son of God, Jesus Christ, our enemy! He will drive us out!" Jesus commanded them to be silent and to cease their frantic gestures. All became quiet and followed Him into the synagogue, to which He had to go from almost one end of the city to the other. There He taught till evening, going out only once to take some refreshment. His theme was, as usual, the nearness of the Kingdom of God and the necessity of Baptism.

+ + +

We offer You, O Lord Jesus, this third
decade in honor of Your proclaiming
the kingdom, and we ask of You,
through this mystery and through
Mary's intercession, the gift of Faith.
Amen.

Our Father, 10 Hail Marys,
Glory Be, O my Jesus.

May the grace of the Mystery of the
Proclamation of the Kingdom come
down into our souls. Amen.

* 4 *

THE
TRANSFIGURATION

*And it came to pass about eight days after these words,
that he took Peter, and James, and John, and went up into
a mountain to pray. And whilst he prayed, the appearance
of his countenance was altered, and his raiment became
white and glittering. And behold two men were talking
with him. And they were Moses and Elias, Appearing
in majesty. And they spoke of his decease that he should
accomplish in Jerusalem. But Peter and those who were
with him were heavy with sleep. And waking, they saw
his glory, and the two men who stood with him.*

LUKE 9:28-32

From the inn near Hadad-Rimmon, Jesus went with
some of the disciples eastward to Kisloth Thabor
which lay at the foot of Thabor toward the south, about
three hours from Rimmon. In the afternoon He sent the

disciples right and left around the mountain, to teach and to cure. Taking with Him Peter, John, and James the Greater, He proceeded up the mountain by a footpath. They spent nearly two hours in ascent, for Jesus paused frequently at the different caves and places made memorable by the sojourn of the Prophets. There He explained to them manifold mysteries and united with them in prayer. They had no provisions, for Jesus had forbidden them to bring any, saying that they should be satiated to overflowing. The view from the summit of the mountain extended far and wide. On it was a large open place surrounded by a wall and shade trees. The ground was covered with aromatic herbs and sweet-scented flowers. Hidden in a rock was a reservoir, which upon the turning of a spigot poured forth water sparkling and very cold. The Apostles washed Jesus' feet and then their own, and refreshed themselves.

Then Jesus withdrew with them into a deep grotto behind a rock which formed, as it were, a door to the cave. It was like the grotto on the Mount of Olives, to which Jesus so often retired to pray, and from it a descent led down into a vault. The sun had set and it was dark, but the Apostles had not remarked the fact, so entrancing were Jesus' words and bearing. He became brighter and brighter, and apparitions of angelic spirits hovered around Him. Peter saw them, for he interrupted Jesus with the question: "Master, what does this mean?"

Jesus answered: "They serve Me!" Peter, quite out of himself, stretched forth his hands, exclaiming: "Master, are we not here? We will serve You in all things!" Jesus began again His instructions, and along with the angelic apparitions flowed alternate streams of delicious perfumes, of celestial delights and contentment over the Apostles. Jesus in the meantime continued to shine with ever-increasing splendor, until He became as if transparent. The circle around them was so lit up in the darkness of night that each little plant could be distinguished on the green sod as if in clear daylight. The three Apostles were so penetrated, so ravished that, when the light reached a certain degree, they covered their heads, prostrated on the ground, and there remained lying.

It was about twelve o'clock at night when I beheld this glory at its height. I saw a shining pathway reaching from Heaven to earth, and on it angelic spirits of different choirs, all in constant movement. Some were small, but of perfect form; others were merely faces peeping forth from the glancing light; some were in priestly garb, while others looked like warriors. Each had some special characteristic different from that of the others, and from each radiated some special refreshment, strength, delight, and light. They were in constant action, constant movement.

The Apostles lay, ravished in ecstasy rather than in sleep, prostrate on their faces. Then I saw three shining figures approaching Jesus in the light. Their coming appeared perfectly natural. It was like that of one who steps from the darkness of night into a place brilliantly illuminated. Two of them appeared in a more definite form, a form more like the corporeal.

They addressed Jesus and conversed with Him. They

were Moses and Elijah. The third apparition spoke no word. It was more ethereal, more spiritual. That was Malachi. I heard Moses and Elijah greet Jesus, and I heard Him speaking to them of His Passion and of Redemption.

Their being together appeared perfectly simple and natural. Moses and Elias did not look aged nor decrepit as when they left the earth. They were, on the contrary, in the bloom of youth. Moses—taller, graver, and more majestic than Elias—had on his forehead something like two projecting bumps. He was clothed in a long garment. He looked like a resolute man, like one who could govern with strictness, though at the same time he bore the impress of purity, rectitude, and simplicity. He told Jesus how rejoiced he was to see Him who had led himself and his people out of Egypt, and who was now once more about to redeem them. He referred to the numerous types of the Savior in his own time, and uttered deeply significant words upon the Paschal lamb and the Lamb of God. Elijah was quite the opposite of Moses. He appeared to be more refined, more lovable, of a sweeter disposition. But both Elias and Moses were very dissimilar from the apparition of Malachi, for in the former one could trace something human, something earthly in form and countenance; yes, there was even a family likeness between them. Malachi, however, looked quite different.

There was in his appearance something supernatural. He looked like an angel, like the personification of strength and repose. He was more tranquil, more spiritual than the others. Jesus spoke with them of all the sufferings He had endured up to the present, and of all that still awaited Him. He related the history of His Passion in detail, point for point. Elijah and Moses frequently expressed their emotion and joy. Their words were full of sympathy and consolation, of reverence for the Savior, and of the uninterrupted praises of God.

They constantly referred to the types of the mysteries of which Jesus was speaking, and praised God for having from all eternity dealt in mercy toward His people. But Malachi kept silence. The disciples raised their heads, gazed long upon the glory of Jesus, and beheld Moses, Elijah, and Malachi. When in describing His Passion Jesus came to His exaltation on the Cross, He extended His arms at the words: "So shall the Son of Man be lifted up!" His face was turned toward the south, He was entirely penetrated with light, and His robe flashed with a bluish white gleam. He, the Prophets, and the three Apostles— all were raised above the earth.

✝ ✝ ✝

We offer You, O Lord Jesus, this
fourth decade in honor of Your
Transfiguration, and we ask of You,
through this mystery and through
Mary's intercession,
the gift of Faith. Amen.

Our Father, 10 Hail Marys,
Glory Be, O my Jesus.

May the grace of the Mystery of the
Transfiguration come down
into our souls. Amen.

* 5 *

INSTITUTION OF
THE HOLY EUCHARIST

For I have received of the Lord that which also I delivered unto you, that the Lord Jesus, the same night in which he was betrayed, took bread, And giving thanks, broke it, and said: Take and eat: this is my body, which shall be delivered for you: do this for the commemoration of me. In like manner also the chalice, after he had supped, saying: This chalice is the new testament in my blood: do this, as often as you shall drink it, for the commemoration of me.

1 CORINTHIANS 9:28-32

At the command of the Lord, the master of the feast again set out the table, which he raised a little higher. It was placed in the middle of the room and covered with a cloth, over which two others were spread, one red, and the other white and transparent.

Then the master set two jugs, one of water, the other of wine, under the table. Peter and John now brought from the back part of the hall, where was the Paschal hearth, the chalice they had brought from Veronica's house. They carried it between them in its case, holding it on their hands, and it looked as if they were carrying a tabernacle. They placed the case on the table before Jesus. The plate with the ribbed Paschal loaves, thin and whitish, stood near under a cover, and the other half of the loaf that had been cut at the Paschal Supper was also on the table. There was a wine and water vessel, also three boxes, one with thick oil, another with liquid oil, and a third empty. A spatula, or flat knife, lay near. The breaking and distributing of bread and drinking out of the same cup were customary in olden times at feasts of welcome and farewell. They were used as signs of brotherly love and friendship. I think there must be something about it in the Scriptures.

Jesus' place was between Peter and John. The doors were closed, for everything was conducted with secrecy and solemnity. When the cover of the chalice had been removed and taken back to the recess in the rear of the Upper Room, Jesus prayed and uttered some very solemn words. I saw that He was explaining the Last Supper to the Apostles, as also the ceremonies that were to accompany it. It reminded me of a priest teaching others the Holy Mass. Jesus then drew from the flat board upon which the vessels stood a kind of shelf, took the white linen that was hanging over the chalice, and spread it on the shelf. I saw Him next take a round, flat plate from the chalice and place it on the covered shelf.

Then taking the loaves from the covered plate nearby, He laid them on the one before Him. The loaves were four-cornered and oblong, in length sufficient to extend beyond the edge of the plate, though narrow enough to allow it to be seen at the sides. Then He drew the chalice somewhat nearer to Himself, took from it the little cup that it contained, and set to the right and left the six smaller vessels that stood around it. He next blessed the Passover loaves and, I think, the oil also that was standing near, elevated the plate of bread with both hands, raised His eyes toward Heaven, prayed, offered, set it down on the table, and again covered it. Then taking the chalice, He received into it wine and water, the former poured by Peter, and the latter by John.

The water He blessed before it was poured into the chalice. He then added a little more water from the small spoon, blessed the chalice, raised it on high, praying and offering, and set it down again. After that Jesus held His hands over the plate upon which the loaves had lain, while at His bidding Peter and John poured water on them; then with the spoon that He had taken from the foot of the chalice. He scooped up some of the water that had flowed over His own hands, and poured it upon theirs. Lastly, that same plate was passed around, and all the Apostles washed their hands in it. I do not know whether these ceremonies were performed in this precise order, but these and all the others that reminded me so much of the Holy Mass, I looked upon with deep emotion. During all this time, Jesus was becoming more and more recollected. He said to the Apostles that He was now about to give them all that He possessed, even His very Self. He seemed to be pouring out His whole Being in love, and I saw Him becoming perfectly transparent. He looked like a luminous apparition.

In profound recollection and prayer, Jesus next broke the bread into several morsels and laid them one over another on the plate. With the tip of His finger, He broke off a scrap from the first morsel and let it fall into the chalice. Again Jesus prayed and taught. His words, glowing with fire and light, came forth from His mouth and entered into all the Apostles, excepting Judas. He took the plate with the morsels of bread, and said, "Take and eat. This is My Body which is given for you." While saying these words, He stretched forth His right hand over it, as if giving a blessing, and as He did so, a brilliant light emanated from Him. His words were luminous as also the Bread, which like a body of light, entered the mouth of the Apostles. It was as if Jesus Himself flowed into them. I saw all of them penetrated with light, bathed in light. Judas alone was in darkness.

Jesus next raised the chalice by its two handles to a level with His face, and pronounced into it the words of consecration. While doing so, He was wholly transfigured and, as it were, transparent. He was as if passing over into what He was giving. He caused Peter and John to drink from the chalice while yet in His hands, and then He set it down.

With the little spoon, John removed some of the Sacred Blood from the chalice to the small cups, which Peter

handed to the Apostles who, two by two, drank from the same cup. Judas also (though of this I am not quite certain) partook of the chalice, but he did not return to his place, for he immediately left the Upper Room. The others thought that Jesus had given him some commission to execute. He left without prayer or thanksgiving. And here we may see what an evil it is to fail to give thanks for our daily bread and for the Bread that endures to life eternal.

The remains of the Sacred Blood in the chalice, the Lord poured into the small cup that fitted into it; then holding His fingers over the chalice, He bade Peter and John to pour water and wine upon them. This ablution He gave to the two to drink from the chalice and, pouring what remained into the smaller cups, passed it down among the rest of the Apostles.

✝ ✝ ✝

We offer You, O Lord Jesus, this fifth
decade in honor of Your Institution
of the Eucharist, and we ask of You,
through this mystery and through
Mary's intercession, the gift of Faith.
Amen.

Our Father, 10 Hail Marys,
Glory Be, O my Jesus.

May the grace of the Mystery of the
Institution of the Eucharist come
down into our souls. Amen.

THE
SORROWFUL
MYSTERIES

* 1 *

THE AGONY
IN THE GARDEN

And going out, he went, according to his custom, to the mount of Olives. And his disciples also followed him. And when he had come to the place, he said to them: Pray, lest you enter into temptation. And he was withdrawn away from them a stone's cast; and kneeling down, he prayed, Saying: Father, if you will, remove this chalice from me: but yet not my will, but yours be done. And there appeared to him an angel from heaven, strengthening him. And being in an agony, he prayed the longer. And his sweat became as drops of blood, trickling down upon the ground.

LUKE 22:39-44

They crossed the brook Cedron, but not by the bridge over which later on Jesus was led bound, for they had taken a byway. Gethsemane on Mount Olivet, to which they were going, was in a direct line one-half hour from the Upper Room, for it was fifteen minutes from the Upper Room to the valley of Josaphat, and the same distance from the latter to Gethsemane. This spot, in which during His last days Jesus had sometimes passed the night with His Apostles and instructed them, consisted of a large pleasure garden surrounded by a hedge. It contained some magnificent shrubbery and a great many fruit trees. Outside the garden were a few deserted houses, open for any that might wish to lodge there. Several persons, as well as the Apostles, had keys to this garden, which was used both as a place of recreation and prayer. Oftentimes, too, people who had no gardens of their own gave there their feasts and entertainments.

There were in it several arbors formed of dense foliage. The Garden of Olives was separated by a road from that of Gethsemane and was higher up the mountain. It was open, being surrounded by only a rampart of earth. It was smaller than the pleasure garden of Gethsemane, a retired corner of the mountain full of grottos, terraces, and olive trees.

Jesus was very sad. He announced to the Apostles the approach of danger, and they became uneasy. Jesus bade eight of them to remain in the Garden of Gethsemane, where there was a kind of summerhouse built of branches and foliage. "Remain here," He said, "while I go to My own place to pray." He took Peter, John, and James the Greater with Him, crossed the road, and went on for a few minutes, until He reached the Garden of Olives farther up the mountain. He was inexpressibly sad, for He felt His approaching agony and temptation. John asked how He, who had always consoled them, could now be so dejected. He replied: "My soul is sorrowful even unto death." He glanced around and on all sides saw anguish and temptation gathering about Him like dense clouds filled with frightful pictures. It was at that moment He said to the three Apostles: "Remain here and watch with Me. Pray lest you enter into temptation!" and they stayed in that place. Jesus went a few steps forward. But the frightful visions pressed around Him to such a degree that, filled with alarm, He turned to the left from the Apostles and plunged down into a grotto formed by an overhanging rock. The Apostles remained in a hollow to the right above. The grotto in which Jesus concealed Himself was about six feet deep. The earth sank gently toward the back, and plants and shrubs hanging from the rocks towering over the entrance made it a place into which no eye could penetrate.

When Jesus left the Apostles, I saw a great number of frightful figures surrounding Him in an ever-narrowing circle. His sorrow and anguish increased.

He withdrew tremblingly into the back of the cave, like one seeking shelter from a violent tempest, and there He prayed. I saw the awful visions following Him into the grotto, and becoming ever more and more distinct. Ah! It was as if that narrow cave encompassed the horrible, the agonizing vision of all the sins, with their delights and their punishments, committed from the Fall of our first parents till the end of the world; for it was here on Mount

Olivet that Adam and Eve, driven from Paradise, had first descended upon the inhospitable earth, and in that very grotto had they in fear and alarm bewailed their misery. I felt in a most lively manner that Jesus, in resigning Himself to the sufferings that awaited Him and sacrificing Himself to Divine Justice in satisfaction for the sins of the world, caused in a certain manner His Divinity to return into the Most Holy Trinity. This He did in order—out of infinite love, in His most pure and sensitive, His most innocent and true Humanity, supported by the love of His human Heart alone—to devote Himself to endure for the sins of the world the greatest excess of agony and pain. To make satisfaction for the origin and development of all kinds of sin and guilty pleasures, the most merciful Jesus, through love for us sinners, received into His own Heart the root of all expiatory reconciliation and saving pains. He allowed those infinite sufferings in satisfaction for endless sins, like a thousand-branched tree of pain, to pierce through, to extend through all the members of His Sacred Body, all the faculties of His holy Soul. Thus entirely given up to His Humanity, He fell on His face, calling upon God in unspeakable sorrow and anguish. He saw in countless forms all the sins of the world with their innate hideousness. He took all upon Himself and offered Himself in His prayer to satisfy the justice of His Heavenly Father for all that guilt by His own sufferings. But Satan who, under a frightful form and with furious mockery, moved around among all this abomination, became at each moment more violently enraged against Him. He evoked before the eyes of His soul visions of the sins of men, one more frightful than the other, and constantly addressed to the Sacred Humanity of Jesus such words as, "What! Will You take this also upon Yourself? Are You ready to endure its penalty? How can you satisfy for this?"

From that point in the heavens in which the sun appears between ten and eleven in the morning, a narrow path of light streamed toward Jesus, and on it I saw a file of angels coming down to Him. They imparted to Him fresh strength and vigor. The rest of the grotto was filled with the frightful and horrible visions of sin, and with the evil spirits mocking and tempting. Jesus took all upon Himself. In the midst of this confusion of abomination, His Heart, the only one that loved God and man perfectly, shrank in terror and anguish from the horror, the burden of all those sins. Ah, I saw there so many things! A whole year would not suffice to relate them!

✢ ✢ ✢

We offer You, O Lord Jesus, this first
decade in honor of Your Agony in the
Garden, and we ask of You, through
this mystery and through Mary's
intercession, the gift of Faith. Amen.

Our Father, 10 Hail Marys,
Glory Be, O my Jesus.

May the grace of the Mystery of the
Agony in the Garden come down
into our souls. Amen.

* 2 *

THE SCOURGING
AT THE PILLAR

He was pierced for our offenses, crushed for our sins. It was our infirmities that He bore, our sufferings, that He endured. Upon Him was the chastisement that makes us whole, by His stripes we are healed.

ISAIAH 53:3-5

Pilate, the base, pusillanimous judge, had several times repeated the cowardly words: "I find no guilt in Him, therefore will I chastise Him and let Him go!" To which the Jews shouted no other response than, "Crucify Him! Crucify Him!" But Pilate, still hoping to carry out his first resolve not to condemn Jesus to death, commanded Him to be scourged after the manner of the Romans. Then the executioners, striking and pushing Jesus with their short staves, led Him through the raging multitude on the forum to the whipping pillar, which stood in front of one of the halls that surrounded the great square to the north of Pilate's palace and not far from the guardhouse. And now came forward to meet Jesus the executioners' servants with their whips, rods, and cords, which they threw down near the pillar. There were six of them, swarthy men all somewhat shorter than Jesus, with coarse, crisp hair, to whom nature had denied a beard other than a thin, short growth like stubble. Their loins were girded and the rest of their clothing consisted of a jacket of leather, or some other wretched stuff, open at the sides, and covering the upper part of the body like a scapular. Their arms were naked, and their feet encased in tattered sandals. The most wicked, the most abject among them were always chosen for the punishment of criminals in the praetorium. These barbarous men had often scourged poor offenders to death at this same pillar. There was something beastly, even devilish, in their appearance, and they were half-intoxicated. Although the Lord was offering no resistance whatever, yet they struck Him with their fists and ropes and with frantic rage dragged Him to the pillar, which stood alone and did not serve as a support to any part of the building.

It was not very high, for a tall man with outstretched arms could reach the top, which was provided with an iron ring. Toward the middle of it on one side were other rings, or hooks. It is impossible to express the barbarity with which those furious hounds outraged Jesus on that short walk to the pillar. They tore from Him Herod's mantle of derision, and almost threw the poor Savior to the ground.

Jesus trembled and shuddered before the pillar. With His own hands, swollen and bloody from the tight cords, and in tremulous haste, He laid aside His garments, while the executioners struck and abused Him. He prayed and implored so touchingly and, for one instant, turned His head toward His most afflicted Mother, who was standing with the holy women in a corner of one of the porches around the square, not far from the scourging place. Turning to the pillar, as if to cover Himself by it, Jesus said: "Turn your eyes from Me!" I know not whether He said these words vocally or mentally, but I saw how Mary took them, for at the same moment, I beheld her turning away and sinking into the arms of the holy women who surrounded her, closely veiled. And now Jesus clasped the pillar in His arms.

The executioners, with horrible imprecations and barbarous pulling, fastened His sacred, upraised hands, by means of a wooden peg, behind the iron ring on top. In thus doing, they so stretched His whole body, that His feet, tightly bound below at the base, scarcely touched the ground. There stood the Holy of Holies, divested of clothing, laden with untold anguish and ignominy, stretched upon the pillar of criminals, while two of the bloodhounds, with sanguinary rage, began to tear with their whips the sacred back from head to foot. The first rods, or scourges, that they used looked as if made of flexible white wood, or they might have been bunches of ox sinews, or strips of hard, white leather.

Our Lord and Savior, the Son of God, true God and

true Man, quivered and writhed like a poor worm under the strokes of the criminals' rods. He cried in a suppressed voice, and a clear, sweet-sounding wailing, like a loving prayer under excruciating torture, formed a touching accompaniment to the hissing strokes of His tormentors. Now and then the cries of the populace and the Pharisees mingled with those pitiful, holy, blessed, plaintive tones like frightful peals of thunder from an angry storm cloud. Many voices cried out together: "Away with Him! Crucify Him!" for Pilate was still negotiating with the people. The uproar was so great that, when he wanted to utter a few words, silence had to be enforced by the flourish of a trumpet. At such moments could be heard the strokes of the rods, the moans of Jesus, the blasphemy of the executioners, and the bleating of the Paschal lambs, which were being washed in the pool near the sheep gate to the east. After this first purification, that they might not again soil themselves, their jaws were muzzled, and they were carried by their owners along the clean road to the Temple. They were then driven around toward the western side, where they were subjected to another ceremonial washing. The helpless bleating of the lambs had in it something indescribably touching. They were the only sounds in unison with the Savior's sighs.

I saw infamous, scantily clad youths at one side of the guardhouse preparing fresh rods, and others going off to seek thorn branches. Some executioners of the High Priests went up to the scourgers and slipped them money, and a large jug of thick, red juice was brought to them, from which they guzzled until they became perfectly furious from intoxication. They had been at work about a quarter of an hour when they ceased to strike, and joined two of the others in drinking. Jesus' body was livid, brown, blue, and red, and entirely covered with swollen cuts. His sacred blood was running down on the ground. He trembled and shuddered. Derision and mockery assailed Him on all sides.

The last two scourgers struck Jesus with whips consisting of small chains, or straps, fastened to an iron handle, the ends furnished with iron points, or hooks. They tore off whole pieces of skin and flesh from His ribs. Oh, who can describe the awful barbarity of that spectacle! But those monsters had not yet satiated their cruelty. They loosened the cords that bound Jesus and turned His back to the pillar and, because He was so exhausted as to be no longer able to stand, they bound Him to it with fine cords passed under His arms across His breast, and below the knees. His hands they fastened to the ring in the middle of the opposite side. Only blood and wounds, only barbarously mangled flesh could be seen on the most sacred, most venerable Body of the Son of God.

✝ ✝ ✝

We offer You, O Lord Jesus, this
second decade in honor of Your
Scourging at the Pillar, and we ask of
You, through this mystery and through
Mary's
intercession, the gift of Faith. Amen.

Our Father, 10 Hail Marys,
Glory Be, O my Jesus.

May the grace of the Mystery of the
Scourging at the Pillar come down
into our souls. Amen.

* 3 *

THE CROWNING
WITH THORNS

*Then therefore, Pilate took Jesus, and scourged him. And
the soldiers plaiting a crown of thorns, put it upon his
head; and they put on him a purple garment. And they
came to him, and said: Hail, king of the Jews; and they
gave him blows. Pilate therefore went forth again, and said
to them: Behold, I bring him forth unto you, that you may
know that I find no cause in him. (Jesus therefore came
forth, bearing the crown of thorns and the purple garment.)
And he said to them: Behold the Man.*

JOHN 19:1-5

The crowning and mocking of Jesus took place in the
inner court of the guardhouse, which stood in the
forum over the prisons. It was surrounded with pillars,
and the entrance was open. There were about fifty low-
lived wretches belonging to the army, jailer's servants,

executioners, lads, slaves, and whipping servants, who took an active part in this maltreatment of Jesus. The mob at first crowded in eagerly, but was soon displaced by the thousand Roman soldiers who surrounded the building. They stood in rank and order, jeering and laughing, thereby giving to Jesus' tormentors new inducement to multiply His sufferings.

Their jokes and laughter encouraged them as applause does the actor. There was a hole in the middle of the court, and to this they had rolled the base of an old column, which may once have stood there. On that base they placed a low, round stool with an upright at the back by which to raise it, and maliciously covered it with sharp stones and potsherds. Once more they tore Jesus' clothing from His wounded body, and threw over Him instead an old red military cloak tattered and so short that it did not reach to the knees. Shreds of yellow tassels hung on it here and there. It was kept in a corner of the executioners' room and used to throw around criminals after their scourging, either to dry the blood or to turn them into derision. Now they dragged Jesus to the stool covered with stones and potsherds, and violently forced His wounded, naked body down upon them.

Then they put upon Him the crown of thorns. It was two hands high, thick, and skillfully plaited, with a projecting edge on top. They laid it like a binder round His brow and fastened it tightly in the back, thus forming it into a crown. It was skillfully woven from thorn branches three fingers thick, the thorns of which grew straight out.

In plaiting the crown, as many of them as possible had been designedly pressed inward.

There were three kinds of thorns, such as with us are called buckthorn, blackthorn, and hawthorn. The projecting edge on top was formed of one kind, which we call blackberry, and it was by this the torturer fastened it on and moved it in order to produce new sufferings. I have seen the spot whence the miscreants brought the thorns. Next they placed in Jesus' hand a thick reed with a tufted top. All this was done with mock solemnity, as if they were really crowning Him king. Then they snatched the reed from His hand and with it struck the crown violently, until His eyes filled with blood. They bent the knee before Him, stuck out their tongue at Him, struck and spat in His face, and cried out: "Hail, King of the Jews!" With shouts of mocking laughter, they upset Him along with the stool, in order to force Him violently down upon it again.

I am not able to repeat all the base inventions employed by those wretches to insult the poor Savior.

Ah! His thirst was horrible, for He was consumed with the fever of His wounds, the laceration caused by the inhuman scourging. He quivered. The flesh on His sides was in many places torn even to the ribs. His tongue contracted convulsively. Only the sacred Blood trickling down from His head washed, as it were in pity, His parched lips which hung languishingly open. Those horrible monsters, seeing this, turned His mouth into a receptacle for their own disgusting filth. Jesus underwent this maltreatment for about half an hour, during which time the cohort surrounding the praetorium in rank and order kept up an uninterrupted jeering and laughing.

And now they again led Jesus, the crown of thorns upon His head, the mock scepter in His fettered hands, the purple mantle thrown around Him, into Pilate's palace. He was unrecognizable on account of the blood that filled His eyes and ran down into His mouth and beard. His body, covered with swollen welts and wounds, resembled a cloth dipped in blood, and His gait was bowed down and tottering. The mantle was so short that He had to stoop in order to cover Himself with it, for at the crowning they had again torn off all His clothing.

Jesus was wearily dragged up the steps, and while He stood a little back, Pilate stepped to the front of the balcony. The trumpet sounded to command attention, for Pilate was going to speak. Addressing the High Priests and the people, he said: "Behold! I bring Him forth to you, that you may know that I find no cause in Him!"

Then Jesus was led forward by the executioners to the front of the balcony where Pilate was standing, so that He could be seen by all the people in the forum. Oh, what a terrible, heart-rending spectacle! Silence, awful and gloomy, fell upon the multitude as they inhumanly treated Jesus, the sacred, martyrized figure of the Son of God, covered with blood and wounds, wearing the frightful crown of thorns, appeared and, from His eyes swimming in blood, cast a glance upon the surging crowd! Nearby stood Pilate, pointing to Him with his finger and crying to the Jews: "Behold the Man!" While Jesus, the scarlet cloak of derision thrown around His lacerated body, His pierced head sinking under the weight of the thorny crown, His fettered hands holding the mock scepter, was standing thus before Pilate's palace, in infinite sadness and benignity, pain and love, like a bloody phantom, exposed to the raging cries of both priests and people, a band of strangers, men and women, their garments girded, crossed the forum and went down to the sheep pool. They were going to help in the washing of the Paschal lambs, whose gentle bleating was still mingling with the sanguinary shouts of the multitude, as if wishing to bear witness to the Silent Truth. Now it was that the true Paschal Lamb of God, the revealed though unrecognized Mystery of this holy day, fulfilled the Prophecies and stretched Himself in silence on the slaughtering bench.

✝ ✝ ✝

We offer You, O Lord Jesus, this third
decade in honor of Your Crowning
with Thorns, and we ask of You,
through this mystery and through
Mary's
intercession, the gift of Faith. Amen.

*Our Father, 10 Hail Marys,
Glory Be, O my Jesus.*

May the grace of the Mystery of the
Crowning with Thorns come down
into our souls. Amen.

* 4 *

THE CARRYING
OF THE CROSS

*And as they led him away, they laid hold of one Simon of
Cyrene, coming from the country; and they laid the cross
on him to carry after Jesus. And there followed him a great
multitude of people, and of women, who bewailed and
lamented him. But Jesus turning to them, said: Daughters
of Jerusalem, weep not over me; but weep for yourselves,
and for your children. For behold, the days shall come,
wherein they will say: Blessed are the barren, and the
wombs that have not borne, and the breasts that have not
nursed. Then shall they begin to say to the mountains: Fall
upon us; and to the hills: Cover us. For if in the green
wood they do these things, what shall be done in the dry?*

LUKE 23:26-31

As soon as the cross was thrown on the ground before
Him, Jesus fell on His knees, put His arms around it,

and kissed it three times while softly uttering a prayer of thanksgiving to His Heavenly Father for the Redemption of mankind now begun. But the executioners dragged Jesus up to a kneeling posture; and with difficulty and little help (and that of the most barbarous kind) He was forced to take the heavy beams upon His right shoulder and hold them fast with His right arm. I saw invisible angels helping Him, otherwise He would have been unable to lift the cross from the ground. As He knelt, He bent under the weight. While Jesus was praying, some of the other executioners placed on the back of the two thieves the arms of their crosses (not yet fastened to the trunk), and tied their upraised hands upon them by means of a stick around which they twisted the cord. These crosspieces were not quite straight, but somewhat curved.

Pilate's horsemen were now ready to start, and the trumpet sounded. They jerked Jesus to His feet, and then fell upon His shoulder the whole weight of the cross, of that cross which, according to His own sacred words of Eternal Truth, we must carry after Him. And now that blessed triumphal procession of the King of Kings, so ignominious upon earth, so glorious in the sight of Heaven, began. Two cords were tied to the end of the cross, and by them two of the executioners held it up, so that it could not be dragged on the ground. Around Jesus, though at some distance, walked the four executioners holding the cords fastened to the fetter-girdle that bound His waist. His mantle was tied up under His arms.

The procession of the Crucifixion was headed by a

trumpeter, who sounded his trumpet at every street corner and proclaimed the execution. Some paces behind him came a crowd of boys and other rude fellows, carrying drink, cords, nails, wedges, and baskets of tools of all kinds, while sturdy servant men bore poles, ladders, and the trunks belonging to the crosses of the thieves. Then followed some of the mounted Pharisees, after whom came a lad bearing on his breast the inscription Pilate had written for the cross. And next came Our Lord and Redeemer, bowed down under the heavy weight of the cross, bruised, torn with scourges, exhausted, and tottering. Since the Last Supper of the preceding evening, without food, drink, and sleep, under continual ill-treatment that might of itself have ended in death, consumed by loss of blood, wounds, fever, thirst, and unutterable interior pain and horror, Jesus walked with tottering steps, His back bent low, His feet naked and bleeding. His hands were bruised and swollen from the cords that had tightly bound them, His face was covered with blood and swellings, His hair and beard were torn and matted with blood, the burden He carried and the fetters pressed the coarse woolen garment into the wounds of His body and the wool stuck fast to those that had been reopened by the tearing off of His clothes. Jeers and malicious words resounded on all sides. He looked unspeakably wretched and tormented, though lovingly resigned.

The two executioners behind Him, who held up the end of the cross by means of ropes fastened to it, increased the toil of Jesus, for they jerked the ropes or let them lie slack, thus moving His burden from side to side. The Roman soldiers in the rear kept the people from swelling its numbers, and they were obliged consequently to plunge down the next bystreet and head off the procession again. Most of them, however, made straight for Golgotha. The executioners pulled Jesus by the cords and pushed Him unmercifully. Then did the Divine Crossbearer fall full length on the ground by the projecting stone, His burden at His side. The drivers, with curses, pulled Him and kicked Him. This brought the procession to a halt, and a tumult arose around Jesus. In vain did He stretch out His hand for someone to help Him. Here and there on the wayside weeping women might be seen, and children whimpering from fear. With the aid of supernatural help, Jesus raised His head, and the terrible, the diabolical wretches, instead of alleviating His sufferings, put the crown of thorns again upon Him. When at last, with all kinds of ill-treatment, they dragged Him up again, they laid the cross once more upon His shoulder.

And now with the greatest difficulty He had to hang His poor head, racked with thorns, to one side in order to be able to carry His heavy load on His shoulder, for the crown was broad. Thus Jesus tottered, with increased torture, up the steep and gradually widening street. The Blessed Mother of Jesus, who shared every suffering of her Son, when the running crowd, the sounding trumpets, and the approach of the soldiers and Pilate's cavalcade announced the commencement of the bitter Way of the Cross, could no longer remain at a distance. She must behold her Divine Son in His sufferings, and she begged John to take her to some place that Jesus would pass. They left, in consequence, the vicinity of Sion, passed the judgment seat, and went through gates and shady walks which were open just now to the people streaming hither and thither, to the western side of a palace which had an arched gateway on the street into which the procession turned after Jesus' first fall.

And now came on the executioner's servants, insolent and triumphant, with their instruments of torture, at the sight of which the Blessed Mother trembled, sobbed, and wrung her hands. One of the men said to the bystanders: "Who is that woman in such distress?" And someone answered: "She is the Mother of the Galilean." When the miscreants heard this, they jeered at the sorrowing Mother in words of scorn, pointed at her with their fingers; and one of the base wretches, snatching up the nails intended for the crucifixion, held them up mockingly before her face.

Wringing her hands, she gazed upon Jesus and, in her anguish, leaned for support against one of the pillars of the gate. She was pale as a corpse, her lips livid. Some of the soldiers were touched. They obliged the Blessed Virgin to retire, but not one of them laid a finger on her. John and the women led her away, and she sank, like one paralyzed in the knees by pain, on one of the cornerstones that supported the wall near the gateway.

✝ ✝ ✝

We offer You, O Lord Jesus, this fourth
decade in honor of Your Carrying of
the Cross, and we ask of You, through
this mystery and through Mary's
intercession, the gift of Faith. Amen.

*Our Father, 10 Hail Marys,
Glory Be, O my Jesus.*

May the grace of the Mystery of the
Carrying of the Cross come down
into our souls. Amen.

* 5 *

THE CRUCIFIXION

*And they came to the place that is called Golgotha, which
is the place of Calvary. And they gave him wine to drink
mingled with gall. And when he had tasted, he would not
drink. And after they had crucified him, they divided his
garments, casting lots; that it might be fulfilled which was
spoken by the prophet, saying: They divided my garments
among them; and upon my vesture they cast lots. Then
were crucified with him two thieves: one on the right hand,
and one on the left. Now from the sixth hour there was
darkness over the whole earth, until the ninth hour.*

MATTHEW 27:33-35; 38-39

There stood the Son of Man, trembling in every limb,
covered with blood and welts; covered with wounds,
some closed, some bleeding; covered with scars and
bruises! He still retained the short woolen scapular over
His chest and back, and the tunic about His loins. The

89

wool of the scapular was dried fast in His wounds and cemented with blood into the new and deep one made by the heavy cross upon His shoulder. This last wound caused Jesus unspeakable suffering. The scapular was now torn ruthlessly from His frightfully lacerated and swollen breast. His shoulder and back were torn to the bone, the white wool of the scapular adhering to the crusts of His wounds and the dried blood on His breast. At last, they tore off His girdle and Jesus, our sweetest Savior, our inexpressibly maltreated Savior, bent over as if trying to hide Himself. As He appeared about to swoon in their hands, they set Him upon a stone that had been rolled nearby, thrust the crown of thorns again upon His head, and offered Him a drink from that other vessel of gall and vinegar. But Jesus turned His head away in silence. And now, when the executioners seized Him by the arms and raised Him in order to throw Him upon the cross, a cry of indignation, loud murmurs and lamentations arose from all His friends.

Jesus was now stretched on the cross by the executioners, He had lain Himself upon it; but they pushed Him lower down into the hollow places, rudely drew His right hand to the hole for the nail in the right arm of the cross, and tied His wrist fast. One knelt on His sacred breast and held the closing hand flat; another placed the long, thick nail, which had been filed to a sharp point, upon the palm of His sacred hand, and struck furious blows with the iron hammer.

After nailing Our Lord's right hand, the crucifiers found that His left, which also was fastened to the cross piece, did not reach to the hole made for the nail, for they had bored a good two inches from the fingertips. They consequently unbound Jesus' arm from the cross, wound cords around it and, with their feet supported firmly against the cross, pulled it forward until the hand reached the hole. Now, kneeling on the arm and chest of the Lord, they fastened the arm again on the beam, and hammered the second nail through the left hand. The blood spurted up and Jesus' sweet, clear cry of agony sounded above the strokes of the heavy hammer.

Both arms had been torn from their sockets, the shoulders were distended and hollow, and at the elbows one could see the disjointed bones. Jesus' breast heaved, and His legs were drawn up doubled to His body. His arms were stretched out in so straight a line that they no longer covered the obliquely rising crosspieces. One could see through the space thus made between them and His armpits. With similar violence the left foot was drawn and fastened tightly with cords over the right; and because it did not rest firmly enough over the right one for nailing, the instep was bored with a fine, flathead piercer, much finer than the one used for the hands.

It was like an auger with a puncher attached. Then seizing the most frightful-looking nail of all, which was much longer than the others, they drove it with great effort through the wounded instep of the left foot and that of the right foot resting below. With a cracking sound, it passed through Jesus' feet into the hole prepared for it in the footblock, and through that again back into the trunk of the cross. I have seen, when standing at the side of the cross, one nail passing through both feet.

Jesus, in unspeakable torture, endured on the cross extreme abandonment and desolation of soul. He prayed to His Heavenly Father in those passages of the Psalms that were now being fulfilled in Himself. I saw around Him angelic figures. He endured in infinite torment all that a poor, crushed, tortured creature, in the greatest abandonment, without consolation human or divine, suffers when faith, hope, and love stand alone in the desert of tribulation, without prospect of return, without taste or sentiment, without a ray of light, left there to live alone.

Jesus wholly abandoned, wholly deprived of all things, and utterly helpless, sacrificed Himself in infinite love. Yes, He turned His abandonment itself into a rich treasure by offering to His Heavenly Father His life, labors, love, and sufferings, along with the bitter sense of our ingratitude that thereby He might strengthen our weakness and enrich our poverty. He made before God His last testament, by which He gave over all His merits to the Church and to sinners. He thought of everyone. In His abandonment He was with every single soul until the end of time.

And so when in His agony He cried out with a loud voice, He meant not only to make known His dereliction, but also to publish to all afflicted souls who acknowledge God as their Father that the privilege of recurring to Him in filial confidence He merited for them then and there. Toward the third hour, Jesus cried in a loud voice: "Eli, Eli, lamma sabacthani!" which means: "My

God! My God! Why have You forsaken Me!" When this clear cry of Our Lord broke the fearful stillness around the cross, the scoffers turned toward it and one said: "He is calling Elijah;" and another: "Let us see whether Elijah will come to deliver Him."

The hour of the Lord was now come. Jesus spoke: "It is consummated!" and raising His head He cried with a loud voice: "Father, into Your hands I commend My Spirit!" The sweet, loud cry rang through Heaven and earth. Then He bowed His head and gave up the ghost. John and the holy women sank, face downward, prostrate on the earth.

We offer You, O Lord Jesus, this fifth decade in honor of Your Crucifixion, and we ask of You, through this mystery and through Mary's intercession, the gift of Faith. Amen.

Our Father, 10 Hail Marys, Glory Be, O my Jesus.

May the grace of the Mystery of the Crucifixion come down into our souls. Amen.

THE
GLORIOUS
MYSTERIES

* 1 *

THE RESURRECTION

And entering into the sepulcher, they saw a young man sitting on the right side, clothed with a white robe: and they were astonished. Who said to them: Be not afraid; you seek Jesus of Nazareth, who was crucified: he is risen, he is not here, behold the place where they laid him. But go, tell his disciples and Peter that he goes before you into Galilee; there you shall see him, as he told you.

MARK 16:5-7

The blessed soul of Jesus in dazzling splendor, between two warrior angels and surrounded by a multitude of resplendent figures, came floating down through the rocky roof of the tomb upon the sacred body. It seemed to incline over it and melt, as it were, into one with it. I saw the sacred limbs moving beneath the swathing bands, and the dazzling, living body of the Lord with His soul

97

and His Divinity coming forth from the side of the winding sheet as if from the wounded Side.

Now I saw the Lord floating in glory up through the rock. The earth trembled, and an angel in warrior garb shot like lightning from Heaven down to the tomb, rolled the stone to one side, and seated himself upon it. The trembling of the earth was so great that the lanterns swung from side to side, and the flames flashed around. The guards fell stunned to the ground and lay there stiff and contorted, as if dead.

The holy women had remained shut up in their house the whole of the preceding day, the Sabbath. They anxiously inquired of one another: "Who will roll away for us the stone from the doors?" Full of longing desire to show the last honors to the sacred body in the tomb, they had entirely lost sight of the stone. They wanted to pour nard water and precious balm over the sacred body and scatter their flowers and aromatic shrubs upon it.

At last the holy women concluded to set the spices on the stone before the tomb and to wait till some disciple would come who would open it for them. And so they went on toward the garden. Outside the tomb the stone was rolled to the right, so that the doors, which were merely lying to, could now be easily opened. The linens in which the sacred body had been enveloped were on the tomb in the following order: the large winding sheet in which it had been wrapped lay undisturbed, only empty and fallen together, containing nothing but the aromatic herbs; the long bandage that had been wound around it was still lying twisted and at full length just as it had been drawn off, on the outer edge of the tomb; but the linen scarf with which Mary had enveloped Jesus' head lay to the right at the head of the tomb.

When, as they approached, the holy women noticed the lanterns of the guard and the soldiers lying around, they became frightened, and went a short distance past the garden toward Golgotha. Magdalen, however, forgetful of danger, hurried into the garden. Salome followed her at some distance, and the other two waited outside.

Magdalen, seeing the guard, stepped back at first a few steps toward Salome, then both made their way together through the soldiers lying around and into the sepulcher. They found the stone rolled away. Magdalen anxiously opened one of them, peered in at the tomb, and saw the linens lying empty and apart. The whole place was resplendent with light, and an angel was sitting at the right of the tomb. Magdalen was exceedingly troubled.

When with beating heart the women entered the sepulcher and drew near the holy tomb, they beheld standing before them the two angels of the tomb in priestly robes, white and shining. The women pressed close to one another in terror and, covering their faces with their hands, bowed tremblingly almost to the ground. One of the angels addressed them. They must not fear, he said, nor must they look for the Crucified here. He was alive, He had arisen, He was no longer among the dead. Then the angel pointed out to them the empty tomb, and ordered them to tell the disciples what they had seen and heard, and that Jesus would go before them into Galilee. The holy women, shaking and trembling with fear, though still full of joy, tearfully gazed at the tomb and the linens, and departed, taking the road toward the gate of execution. They were still very much frightened.

Meanwhile Magdalen was alone, she was afraid to enter the sepulcher at once, so she waited out on the step at the entrance. She stooped down, trying to see through the low doors into the cave and even as far as the stone couch. She saw the two angels in white priestly garments sitting at the head and the foot of the tomb, and heard the words: "Woman, why do you weep?" She cried out in her grief: "They have taken my Lord away! I know not where they have laid Him!" Saying this and seeing nothing but the linens, she turned weeping, like one seeking something, and as if she must find Him. She had a dim presentiment that Jesus was near, and even the apparition of the angels could not turn her from her one idea. She did not appear conscious of the fact that it was an angel that spoke to her. She thought only of Jesus; her only thought was: "Jesus is not here! Where is Jesus?" I saw her running a few steps from the sepulcher and then returning like one half-distracted and in quest of something.

About ten steps from the sepulcher and toward the east, where the garden rose in the direction of the city, she spied in the gray light of dawn, standing among the bushes behind a palm tree, a figure clothed in a long, white garment. Rushing toward it, she heard once more the words: "Woman, why do you weep? Whom do you seek?" She thought it was the gardener. I saw that he had a spade in his hand and on his head a flat hat, which had a piece of something like bark standing out in front, as a protection from the sun. At the words: "Whom do you seek?" Magdalen at once answered: "Sir, if you have taken Him from here, show me where you have laid Him! I will take Him away!" And she again glanced around, as if to see whether he had not laid Him someplace near. Then Jesus, in His well-known voice, said: "Mary!" Recognizing the voice, and forgetting the crucifixion, death, and burial now that He was alive, she turned quickly and, as once before, exclaimed: "Rabboni!" (Master!). She fell on her knees before Him and stretched out her arms toward His feet. But Jesus raised His hand to keep her off, saying: "Do not touch Me, for I have not yet ascended to My Father. But go to My brethren, and say to them: I ascend to My Father and to your Father, to My God and to your God." At these words the Lord vanished. It was explained to me why Jesus said: "Do not touch Me," but I have only an indistinct remembrance of it. I think He said it because Magdalen was so impetuous. She seemed possessed of the idea that Jesus was alive just as He was before, and that everything was as it used to be.

✝ ✝ ✝

We offer You, O Lord Jesus, this first
decade in honor of Your Resurrection,
and we ask of You, through this mystery and through Mary's intercession,
the gift of Faith. Amen.

*Our Father, 10 Hail Marys,
Glory Be, O my Jesus.*

May the grace of the Mystery of the
Resurrection come down into
our souls. Amen.

* 2 *

THE ASCENSION

And the Lord Jesus, after he had spoken to them,
was taken up into heaven, and sits on the right hand
of God. But they going forth preached everywhere:
the Lord working with them, and confirming
the word with signs that followed.

MARK 16:19-20

Jesus communicated with the Apostles quite naturally in those last days. He ate and prayed with them, walked with them in many directions, and repeated all that He had before told them. When Jesus was walking with the Apostles around Jerusalem, some of the Jews perceived the apparition, and were terrified. They ran to hide themselves, or to shut themselves up in their houses. Even the Apostles and disciples accompanied Him with a certain degree of timidity, for there was in Him something too spiritual for them. Jesus appeared also in other places,

Bethlehem and Nazareth for instance, to those especially with whom He and His Blessed Mother had formerly spoken. He scattered blessings everywhere, and those who saw Him believed and joined the Apostles and disciples.

On the night before His wonderful Ascension, I saw Jesus in the inner hall of the house of the Last Supper with the Blessed Virgin and The Eleven. The disciples and the holy women were praying in the side halls. At the dawn of day Jesus left the house of the Last Supper with The Eleven. The Blessed Virgin followed them closely; the disciples, at some little distance. They passed through the streets of Jerusalem where all was quiet, the inhabitants still buried in sleep. I recognized the route that they took as that of the Palm Sunday procession.

I saw that Jesus went with them over all the paths trodden by Him during His Passion, in order to inspire them by His teachings and admonitions with a lively appreciation of the fulfillment of the Promise. In every place in which some scene of His Passion had been enacted, He paused a moment to instruct them upon the accomplishment of the words of the Prophets, upon the Promises, and to explain the symbolical relation of the place to the same. On those sites which the Jews had laid waste, over which they had thrown heaps of stones, through which they had opened ditches, or which they had rendered impassable in other ways in order to prevent their being venerated, Jesus ordered the disciples in His train to go on ahead and clear away all obstructions, which they quickly did. Then bowing low as He passed, they allowed Him to take the lead again while they followed. Just before the gate that led out to Mount Calvary, they turned aside from the road to a delightful spot shaded by trees. It was one of several places of prayer that lay around Jerusalem.

Jesus paused to teach and comfort the little flock. Meanwhile, day dawned brightly; their hearts grew lighter, and they even began to think that Jesus would still remain with them. New crowds of believers arrived, but I saw no women among them. Jesus paused awhile with the crowd in an exceedingly cool and lovely spot covered with beautiful long grass; I was surprised to see that it was nowhere trodden down. The multitude that here surrounded Jesus was so great that I could no longer count them.

Jesus spoke to them a very long time, like one who is about closing his discourse and coming to a conclusion. His hearers divined that the hour of parting was near, and yet they had no idea that the time still intervening was to be so short. The sun was already high, was already far above the horizon. I know not whether I express it rightly, for in that country it seems to me the sun is not so high as it is here. It always appears to me as if it were nearer to one. I do not see it as here, rising like a small globe. It shines there with far more brilliancy. Its rays are, on the whole, not so fine. They often look like a broad pathway of light. Jesus and His followers tarried here fully an hour. By this time the people in Jerusalem were all on the alert, amazed at the crowds of people they descried around Mount Olivet. Out of the city, too, crowds were pouring in bands. They consisted of all who had gone out to meet Jesus on Palm Sunday. The narrow roads were soon thronged, though around Jesus and His own, the space was left free. The Lord went only to Gethsemane and from the Garden of Olives up to the summit of the mount.

The crowd followed as in a procession, ascending by the different paths that encircled the mount. Many even pressed through the fences and garden hedges. Jesus at each instant shone more brightly and His motions became more rapid. The disciples hastened after Him, but it was impossible to overtake Him. When He reached the top of the mountain, He was resplendent as a beam of white sunlight. A shining circle, glancing in all the colors of the rainbow, fell from Heaven around Him. The pressing crowd stood in a wide circle outside, as if blending with it. Jesus Himself shone still more brightly than the glory about Him. He laid the left hand on His breast and, raising the right, turned slowly around, blessing the whole world. The crowd stood motionless. I saw all receive the benediction. Jesus did not impart it with the flat, open hand, like the rabbis, but like the Christian Bishops. With great joy I felt His blessing of the whole world.

And now the rays of light from above united with the glory emanating from Jesus, and I saw Him disappearing, dissolving as it were in the light from Heaven, vanishing as He rose. It appeared as if one sun was lost in another, as if one flame entered another, as if a spark floated into a flame. It was as if one were gazing into the full midday splendors of the sun, though this light was whiter and clearer. Full day compared with this would be dark. First, I lost sight of Jesus' head, then His whole person, and lastly His feet, radiant with light, disappeared in the celestial glory. I saw innumerable souls from all sides going into that light and vanishing on high with the Lord, and He disappeared as it were in a cloud of light. Out of that cloud, something like dew, like a shower of light fell upon all below, and when they could no longer endure the splendor, they were seized with amazement and terror. The Apostles and disciples, who were nearest to Jesus, were blinded by the dazzling glare. They were forced to lower their eyes, while many cast themselves prostrate on their faces.

+ + +

We offer You, O Lord Jesus, this second decade in honor of Your Ascension,
and we ask of You, through this mystery and through Mary's intercession, the gift of Faith. Amen.

Our Father, 10 Hail Marys,
Glory Be, O my Jesus.

May the grace of the Mystery of the Ascension come down into our souls. Amen.

* 3 *

THE DESCENT OF
THE HOLY SPIRIT
ON PENTECOST

*And when the days of the Pentecost were accomplished,
they were all together in one place: And suddenly there
came a sound from heaven, as of a mighty wind coming,
and it filled the whole house where they were sitting. And
there appeared to them parted tongues as it were of fire,
and it sat upon every one of them. And they were all filled
with the Holy Spirit, and they began to speak with various
tongues, according as the Holy Spirit gave them to speak.*

ACTS OF THE APOSTLES, 2:1-4

The whole interior of the Last Supper room was, on the
eve of the feast of Pentecost, ornamented with green
bushes in whose branches were placed vases of flowers.
Garlands of green were looped from side to side. The

screens that cut off the side halls and the vestibule were removed; only the gate of the outer court was closed. Peter in his episcopal robe stood at a table covered with red and white under the lamp in front of the curtained Holy of Holies. On the table lay rolls of writing. Opposite him in the doorway leading from the entrance hall stood the Blessed Virgin, her face veiled, and behind her in the entrance hall stood the holy women. The Apostles stood in two rows turned toward Peter along either side of the hall, and from the side halls, the disciples ranged behind the Apostles took part in the hymns and prayers. When Peter broke and distributed the bread that he had previously blessed, first to the Blessed Virgin, then to the Apostles and disciples who stepped forward to receive it, they kissed his hand, the Blessed Virgin included.

After midnight there arose a wonderful movement in all nature. It communicated itself to all present as they stood in deep recollection, their arms crossed on their breast, near the pillars of the Supper Room and in the side halls, silently praying. Stillness pervaded the house, and silence reigned throughout the whole enclosure.

Toward morning I saw above the Mount of Olives a glittering white cloud of light coming down from Heaven and drawing near to the house. In the distance it appeared to me like a round ball borne along on a soft, warm breeze. But coming nearer, it looked larger and floated over the city like a luminous mass of fog until it stood above Sion and the house of the Last Supper. It seemed to contract and to shine with constantly increasing brightness, until at last with a rushing, roaring noise as of wind, it sank like a thunder cloud floating low in the atmosphere.

The luminous cloud descended low over the house, and with the increasing sound, the light became brighter. I saw the house and its surroundings more clearly, while the Apostles, the disciples, and the women became more and more silent, more deeply recollected. Afterward there shot from the rushing cloud streams of white light down upon the house and its surroundings. The streams intersected one another in sevenfold rays, and below each intersection resolved into fine threads of light and fiery drops. The point at which the seven streams intersected was surrounded by a rainbow light, in which floated a luminous figure with outstretched wings, or rays of light that looked like wings, attached to the shoulders. In that same instant the whole house and its surroundings were penetrated through and through with light. The five-branched lamp no longer shone.

The sacred fire was poured forth also upon the disciples and the women present in the antechamber, and thus the resplendent cloud gradually dissolved as if in a rain of light. The flames descended on each in different colors and in different degrees of intensity. After that effusion of heavenly light, a joyous courage pervaded the assembly. All were full of emotion, and as if intoxicated with joy and confidence. They gathered around the Blessed Virgin who was, I saw, the only one perfectly calm, the only one that retained a quiet, holy self-possession.

They gave thanks and praised God with great

emotion. The light meanwhile vanished. Peter delivered an instruction to the disciples, and sent several of them out to the inns of the Pentecost guests. Between the house of the Last Supper and the Pool of Bethsaida there were several sheds and public lodging houses for the accommodation of guests who came up for the feast. They were at this time very numerous, and they too received the grace of the Holy Ghost. An extraordinary movement pervaded all nature. Good people were roused interiorly, while the wicked became timid, uneasy, and still more stiff-necked. They had become, by all that they had seen and heard, quite intimate and kindly disposed toward the disciples, so that the latter, intoxicated with joy, announced to them the Promise of the Holy Spirit as fulfilled. Then too did they become conscious of a change within their own souls and, at the summons of the disciples, they gathered around the Pool of Bethsaida.

In the house of the Last Supper, Peter imposed hands on five of the Apostles who were to help to teach and baptize at the Pool of Bethsaida. They were James the Less, Bartholomew, Mathias, Thomas, and Jude Thaddeus. The last-named had a vision during his ordination. It seemed to him that he was clasping to his breast the Body of the Lord.

Before departing for the Pool of Bethsaida to consecrate the water and administer Baptism, they received on their knees the benediction of the Blessed Virgin. Before Jesus' Ascension, this ceremony was performed standing.

On the following days I saw this blessing given whenever the Apostles left the house, and also on their return.

Baptism at the Pool of Bethsaida had been arranged by Jesus Himself for this day's feast, and the disciples had, in consequence, made all kinds of preparations at the pool, as well as in the old synagogue that they had appropriated for their own use. The walls of the synagogue were hung with tapestry, and from the building down to the pool a covered tent-way was erected.

The Apostles and disciples went in solemn procession, two by two, from the house of the Last Supper to the Pool. Some of the disciples carried a leathern bottle of holy water and an asperges. The five Apostles upon whom Peter had imposed hands separated, each taking one of the five entrances to the pool, and addressed the people with great enthusiasm. Peter stepped upon the teacher's chair that had been prepared for him in the third circle of the Pool, counting from the outside one. This terrace was the broadest. The hearers filled all the terraces of the pool. When the Apostles spoke, the multitude hearkened in amazement, for everyone listened to what sounded to him his own language. It was owing to this astonishment of the people that Peter lifted up his voice, as is recorded in the Acts of the Apostles. (Acts 2:14-40).

✝ ✝ ✝

We offer You, O Lord Jesus, this third
decade in honor of Pentecost, and we
ask of You, through this mystery and
through Mary's intercession,
the gift of Faith. Amen.

Our Father, 10 Hail Marys,
Glory Be, O my Jesus.

May the grace of the Mystery of
Pentecost come down into
our souls. Amen.

* 4 *

THE ASSUMPTION
OF THE BLESSED
VIRGIN MARY

And a great sign appeared in heaven:
A woman clothed with the sun, and the moon under
her feet, and on her head a crown of twelve stars.

APOCALYPSE 12:1

Peter bore the Blessed Sacrament to Mary in the cross
hanging on his breast, and John carried on a shallow
dish the chalice containing the Most Sacred Blood. This
chalice was white, small as if for pouring, and of the same
shape as that used at the Last Supper. Its stem was so short
that it could be held with two fingers only. Thaddeus now
brought forward a little incense basin. Peter first gave the
Blessed Virgin the last anointing, just as that Sacrament
is administered at the present day. Next he administered
Holy Communion, which she received sitting up without

support. Then she sank back again on her pillow, and after the Apostles had offered a short prayer, she received the chalice from John, but not now in so upright a posture.

After Communion, Mary spoke no more. Her countenance, blooming and smiling as in youth, was raised above. A pathway of light arose from Mary up to the heavenly Jerusalem, up to the throne of the Most Holy Trinity. On either side of this pathway I saw clouds of light out of which gazed angelic faces. Mary raised her arms to the Heavenly Jerusalem. Her body with all its wrappings was floating so high above the couch that I could see under it. The two choirs of angels united under this figure and soared up with it, as if separating it from the body, which now sank back upon the couch, the hands crossed upon the breast. She soared to her Son, whose Wounds were flashing light far more brilliant than that which surrounded Him.

He received her and placed in her hand a scepter, pointing at the same time over the whole circumference of the earth. At last I saw, and the sight filled me with joy, a multitude of souls released from Purgatory and soaring up to Heaven, and I received the surety that every year, on the feast of Mary's Assumption, many of her devout clients are freed from Purgatory. The hour of Mary's death was made known to me as that of None, at which time also Jesus had died on the cross. The body of the Blessed Virgin lay radiant with light upon the couch, the eyes closed, the hands crossed upon the breast. All present knelt, adoring God.

The holy body was laid in a coffin of snow-white wood with a tightly fitting, arched cover, which was fastened down at the head, the foot, and in the middle, with gray straps. The coffin was then laid on a litter. Everything was done with the utmost solemnity, and all were penetrated with deep emotion. The sorrow of the mourners was more human and more openly expressed than at Jesus' burial, at which holy awe and reverence predominated. When it was time to bear the coffin to the grotto, one half-hour distant, Peter and John raised it from the litter and carried it in their hands to the door of the house, outside of which it was again laid on the litter, which Peter and John then raised upon their shoulders. Six of the Apostles thus carried it in turn.

Before reaching the grotto, the litter was set down. Four of the Apostles bore the coffin in, and placed it in the hollow of the tomb. All went, one by one, into the grotto, where they knelt in prayer before the holy body, honoring it and taking leave of it. Then the tomb was shut in by a wicker screen that extended from the front edge of the tomb to the top of the vaulted wall above. Before the entrance of the grotto they made a trench, which they planted so thickly with blooming flowers and bushes covered with berries that one could gain access to it only from the side, and that only by making his way through the underwood.

On the night following the burial took place the bodily Assumption of the Blessed Virgin into Heaven. I saw on this night several of the Apostles and holy women in the little garden, praying and singing Psalms before the grotto. I saw a broad pathway of light descend from Heaven and rest upon the tomb. In it were circles of glory full of angels, in the midst of whom the resplendent soul of the Blessed Virgin came floating down. Before her went her Divine Son, the marks of His Wounds flashing with light. In the innermost circle, that which surrounded the holy soul of Mary, the angels appeared like the faces of very young children; in the second circle, they were like those of children from six to eight years old; and in the outermost, like the faces of youths, I could clearly distinguish only the face, the rest of the figure consisting of perfectly transparent light. Encircling the head of the Blessed Virgin like a crown, was a choir of blessed spirits. The blessed soul of Mary, floating before Jesus, penetrated through the rock and into the tomb, out of which she again arose radiant with light in her glorified body and, escorted by the entire multitude of celestial spirits, returned in triumph to the heavenly Jerusalem.

Next day, when the Apostles were engaged in choir service, Thomas made his appearance with two companions. Thomas was greatly grieved when he heard that the Blessed Virgin was already buried. He wept with an abundance of tears quite astonishing to behold, for he could not forgive himself for coming so late. Weeping bitterly he threw himself on the spot upon which the blessed soul of Mary had left her body, and afterward knelt long before the altar.

The Apostles, who had not interrupted their choir-chanting on account of his coming, now gathered around him, raised him up, embraced him, and set before him and his companions bread, honey, and some kind of beverage in little jugs. After that they accompanied him with lights to the tomb. Two disciples bent the shrubbery to one side. Thomas went in and prayed before the coffin. Then John loosened the three straps that bound it, for it rose high enough above the trough-like couch to admit of being opened. They stood the lid of the coffin on one side and, to their intense astonishment, beheld only the empty winding sheets lying like a husk, or shell, and in perfect order. Only over the face was it drawn apart, and over the breast slightly opened. The swathing bands of the arms and hands lay separate, as if gently drawn off, but in perfect order. The Apostles gazed in amazement, their hands raised. John cried out: "She is no longer here!" The others came in quickly, wept, prayed. Then rising, they took the winding sheet just as it was, all the grave linens, and the coffin to keep as relics, and returned to the house by the Holy Way, praying and singing Psalms.

We offer You, O Lord Jesus, this fourth decade in honor of The Assumption, and we ask of You, through this mystery and through Mary's intercession, the gift of Faith. Amen.

Our Father, 10 Hail Marys, Glory Be, O my Jesus.

May the grace of the Mystery of the Assumption come down into our souls. Amen.

* 5 *

THE CORONATION
OF THE BLESSED
VIRGIN MARY

*You are the glory of Jerusalem,
you are the joy of Israel, you
are the honor of our people.*

JUDITH 15:10

Our Redeemer Jesus entered heaven leading the purest soul of his Mother at His right hand. She alone of all mortals deserved exemption from particular judgment. For Her there was none, and no account was asked or demanded of her for what She had received; for such was the promise that had been given to her, when She was exempted from the common guilt and chosen as the Queen privileged above the laws of the children of Adam. For the same reason, instead of being judged with the rest, she shall be seated at the right hand of the Judge to judge with Him all creatures. If in the first instant of her Conception she was the brightest Aurora, effulgent with the rays of the sun of the Divinity beyond all the brightness of the most exalted seraphim, and if afterwards she was still further illumined by the contact of the hypostatic Word, who derived his humanity from her purest substance, this is why it is necessarily fitting that she should be His Companion for all eternity. She possessed such a likeness to Him, that none greater can be possible between a Godman and a creature. In this light the Redeemer Himself presented her before the throne of the Divinity. Speaking to the eternal Father in the presence of all the blessed, who were enthralled at this wonder, the most sacred humanity uttered these words:

"Eternal Father, my most beloved Mother, Your beloved daughter and the cherished Spouse of the Holy Spirit, now comes to take possession of the crown and glory, which We have prepared as a reward for her merit. She is the one who was born as the rose among thorns, untouched, pure and beautiful, worthy of being embraced by Us and of being placed upon a throne to which none of our creatures can ever attain, and to which those conceived in sin cannot aspire. This is our chosen and our only one, distinguished above all else, to whom We communicated our grace and our perfections beyond the measure accorded to other creatures; in whom We have deposited the treasure of our incomprehensible Divinity and its gifts; who most faithfully preserved and made fruitful the talents which We gave her; who never swerved from our will, and who found grace and pleasure in our eyes. My Father, most fair is the tribunal of our justice and mercy, and in it the services of our friends are repaid in the most superabundant manner. It is right that to my Mother be given the reward of a Mother. If during her whole life and in all her works she was as like to Me as is possible for a creature to be, let her also be as like to Me in glory and on the throne of our Majesty, so that where holiness is in essence, there it may also be found in its highest participation."

This decree of the incarnate Word was approved by the Father and the Holy Ghost. The most holy soul of Mary was immediately raised to the right hand of her Son and true God, and placed on the royal throne of the most holy Trinity, which neither men, nor angels nor the seraphim themselves attain, and will not attain for all eternity. This is the most exalted and superior privilege of our Queen and Lady, that she is seated on the throne with the three divine Persons and holds her place as Empress. To the eminence and majesty of that position, inaccessible to all other creatures, correspond her gifts of glory, comprehension, vision and fruition, because She enjoys, above all and more than all, the infinite Object, which the other blessed enjoy in an endless variety of degrees. She knows, penetrates, and understands much deeper the eternal Being and its infinite attributes. Moreover, she lovingly delights in its mysteries and most hidden secrets, more than all the rest of the blessed. Just the same, there is an infinite distance between the glory of the divine Persons and that of the most holy Mary; for the light of the Divinity, as says the Apostle (1 Timothy 6:16), is inaccessible and in it alone dwells immortality and glory by essence. Although the most holy soul of Christ also exceeds without measure the gifts of his Mother, yet the great Queen surpasses inaccessibly all the saints in glory, and has a likeness to that of Christ, which cannot be understood in this life, nor ever described.

Just as little can be explained, so also the extra joy that the blessed experienced on that day in singing the new songs of praise to the Omnipotent and in celebrating the glory of his Daughter, the Mother and Spouse are indescribable. For in Her He had exalted all the works of his right hand. Although to the Lord himself could come no new or essential glory, because He possessed and possesses it immutably infinite through all eternity; yet the exterior manifestations of his pleasure and satisfaction at the fulfillment of his eternal decrees were greater on that day, and from the throne a voice, as if of the eternal Father, resounded, saying:

"In the glory of our beloved and most loving Daughter all the pleasure of our holy will is fulfilled to our entire satisfaction. To all the creatures We have given existence, creating them out of nothing, in order that they may participate in our infinite goods and treasures according to the inclination and pleasure of our immense bounty. The very ones who were made capable of our grace and glory, have abused this blessing. Our cherished

Daughter alone had no part in the disobedience and sin of the rest, and she has earned what the unworthy children of perdition have despised. Our heart has not been disappointed in her at any time or moment. To her belong the rewards, which according to our conditional decree We had prepared for the disobedient angels and for their followers among men, if they had been faithful to their grace and vocation. She has recompensed Us for their falling away by her subjection and obedience; she has pleased Us in all her operations and has merited a seat on the throne of our Majesty."

✛ ✛ ✛

We offer You, O Lord Jesus, this fifth decade in honor of The Coronation, and we ask of You, through this mystery and through Mary's intercession, the gift of Faith. Amen.

Our Father, 10 Hail Marys,
Glory Be, O my Jesus.

May the grace of the Mystery of the Coronation come down into our souls. Amen.

HOW TO PRAY
THE ROSARY

THE MYSTERIES OF THE ROSARY

To be meditated upon while praying the Rosary.

THE JOYFUL MYSTERIES

Said on Mondays and Saturdays; and on Sundays from the First Sunday of Advent until the Baptism of the Lord.

1st JOYFUL MYSTERY: The Annunciation

2nd JOYFUL MYSTERY: The Visitation

3rd JOYFUL MYSTERY: The Nativity

4th JOYFUL MYSTERY: The Presentation in the Temple

5th JOYFUL MYSTERY: The Finding in the Temple

THE LUMINOUS MYSTERIES

Said on Thursdays.

1st LUMINOUS MYSTERY: The Baptism of Jesus

2nd LUMINOUS MYSTERY: The Wedding at Cana

3rd LUMINOUS MYSTERY: Proclamation of the Kingdom

4th LUMINOUS MYSTERY: The Transfiguration

5th LUMINOUS MYSTERY: Institution of the Holy Eucharist

THE SORROWFUL MYSTERIES

Said on Tuesdays and Fridays; and on the Sundays of Lent.

1st SORROWFUL MYSTERY: The Agony in the Garden

2nd SORROWFUL MYSTERY: The Scourging at the Pillar

3rd SORROWFUL MYSTERY: The Crowning with Thorns

4th SORROWFUL MYSTERY: The Carrying of the Cross

5th SORROWFUL MYSTERY: The Crucifixion

THE GLORIOUS MYSTERIES

Said on Wednesdays; and all Sundays in Ordinary Time.

1st GLORIOUS MYSTERY: The Resurrection

2nd GLORIOUS MYSTERY: The Ascension

3rd GLORIOUS MYSTERY: The Descent of the Holy Spirit on
Pentecost

4th GLORIOUS MYSTERY: The Assumption of the Blessed
Virgin Mary

5th GLORIOUS MYSTERY: The Coronation of the Blessed
Virgin Mary

HOW TO PRAY
THE ROSARY

1. Make the Sign of the Cross and say The Apostles' Creed.

2. Say the Our Father.

3. Say 3 Hail Marys.

4. Say the Glory Be.

5. Announce the First Mystery; then say the Our Father.

6. Say 10 Hail Marys.

7. Say the Glory Be.

8. Say the O my Jesus.

9. Announce the Second Mystery; then say the Our Father, 10 Hail Mary's, Glory Be and O my Jesus.

10. Announce the Third Mystery; then say the Our Father, 10 Hail Marys, Glory Be and O my Jesus.

11. Announce the Fourth Mystery; then say the Our Father, 10 Hail Marys, Glory Be and O my Jesus.

12. Announce the Fifth Mystery; then say the Our Father, 10 Hail Marys, Glory Be and O my Jesus.

13. Conclude by saying the Hail, Holy Queen.

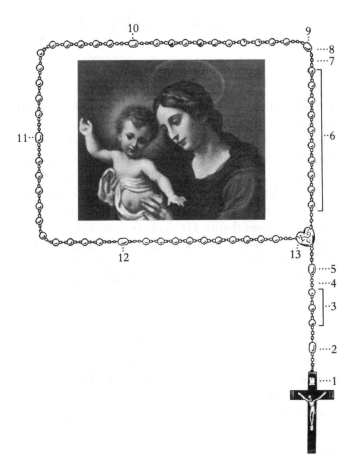

ROSARY PRAYERS

THE APOSTLES' CREED

I BELIEVE in God, the Father Almighty, Creator of heaven and earth; and in Jesus Christ, His only Son, our Lord; who was conceived by the Holy Ghost, born of the Virgin Mary, suffered under Pontius Pilate, was crucified, died, and was buried. He descended into Hell; the third day He arose again from the dead;He ascended into Heaven, sitteth at the right hand of God, the Father Almighty; from thence He shall come to judge the living and the dead. I believe in the Holy Ghost, the Holy Catholic Church, the Communion of Saints, the forgiveness of sins, the resurrection of the body, and life everlasting. Amen.

OUR FATHER

OUR FATHER, Who art in Heaven, hallowed be Thy Name. Thy kingdom come, Thy will be done on earth as it is in Heaven. Give us this day our daily bread, and forgive us our trespasses, as we forgive those who trespass against us. And lead us not into temptation, but deliver us from evil. Amen.

HAIL MARY

HAIL MARY, full of grace, the Lord is with thee; blessed art thou among women, and blessed is the fruit of thy womb, Jesus. Holy Mary, Mother of God, pray for us sinners, now and at the hour of our death. Amen.

GLORY BE

GLORY BE to the Father, and to the Son, and to the Holy Ghost. As it was in the beginning, is now, and ever shall be, world without end. Amen.

O MY JESUS

*To be said after the Glory Be following each decade
of the Rosary. All pray it together.*

O MY JESUS, forgive us our sins, save us from the fires of Hell, lead all souls to Heaven, especially those who are in most need of Thy mercy.

THE HAIL, HOLY QUEEN

HAIL, HOLY QUEEN, Mother of mercy, our life, our sweetness and our hope. To thee do we cry, poor banished children of Eve. To thee do we send up our sighs, mourning and weeping in this valley of tears. Turn then, most gracious advocate, thine eyes of mercy toward us. And after this our exile, show unto us the blessed Fruit of thy womb, Jesus. O clement, O loving, O sweet Virgin Mary.

V. Pray for us, O holy Mother of God.

R. That we may be made worthy of the promises of Christ.

Note: When the Rosary is said aloud by two or more persons, one person is the leader; he says the first part of each prayer, and everyone else answers by saying the remainder of the prayer. The O My Jesus and the body of the Hail, Holy Queen are said by all together.